# HOOP-LA!

## KIRSTY NEALE

# D&C
David and Charles

www.stitchcraftcreate.co.uk

# CONTENTS

# INTRODUCTION

One of the things I love most about the internet is how quickly it can spread a good idea. Framing a piece of embroidery or an appliquéd picture used to be a tricky and often prohibitively expensive business. The concept of framing an unembellished piece of fabric just because you liked the pattern was pretty much out of the question. I'm not sure when I first noticed people sharing pictures of embroidery displayed in the same hoop used to stitch it, but right from the start it seemed like the smartest of solutions.

Over the last few years, this idea has grown to be not just popular but seemingly the standard way of displaying fabric-based art. However, something that often surprises me is how rarely the hoops themselves are decorated. It's not so much that plain wood is unattractive but more often that it is uninteresting. So, alongside 100 fabric-based projects, this book also includes a section on decorating embroidery hoops – from simple techniques like painting and staining, to more elaborate options including collage and crochet.

While most of the projects show off one of these hoop treatments, the idea is that you're free to mix and match. Take your favourite appliqué design and frame it in a collaged hoop instead of a painted one. If you can't crochet, swap yarn for a fancy lace trim. You can also mix things up when decorating the hoops, maybe yarn-wrapping sections of a wood-stained frame or combining paint and decorative tape. Think of the ideas as a recipe, blending different ingredients to create projects that perfectly suit your style and skills.

However you use the ideas, I hope you'll be inspired to create beautiful projects that you're proud to display in a smarter-than-average embroidery hoop.

5

# MATERIALS AND EQUIPMENT

You may already have many of the tools needed for general sewing and crafting projects. The list given here covers those needed to make the projects in this book.

## Materials

**Fabric.** Plain and patterned, new or vintage, in just about any colour or weight you want to try.

**Felt.** For covering the back of hoops, as well as using in projects.

**Fusible web.** This is a type of heat-activated dry adhesive, sold in sheets with a paper backing and used to join two pieces of fabric together. It's often sold under a brand name such as Bondaweb, Heat'n'Bond or Wonder Under.

**Interfacing.** Fusible (iron-on) in medium and heavy weights.

**Paper.** For collage, e.g. patterned tissue, gift wrap, old book pages, scraps torn from magazines or catalogues.

**Ribbon, braid, lace and other fancy trims.** Short lengths of various trims will be useful for some of the projects.

**Threads.** Stranded embroidery threads and reels of sewing cotton.

**Yarn.** For wrapping and crochet.

## Equipment

**Wooden embroidery hoops.** Various sizes, round or oval.

**Scissors.** A small pair for threads and embroidery, a large pair for cutting fabric and a separate pair for cutting paper or card.

**Needles.** Embroidery needles, sharps for general stitching, crewel or tapestry needles for stitching with yarn.

**Pins.** Dressmaker's pins for temporarily fixing fabric pieces together.

**Erasable fabric marker pen.** For transferring patterns onto fabric. Remove the lines with water and a small paintbrush, or alcohol-free baby wipes.

**Ruler and/or tape measure.** A normal desk ruler and standard tape measure will be fine.

**Screwdriver.** For adjusting and tightening the hoop screw.

**Pencil and tracing paper.** For copying and transferring templates.

**Adhesives.** Fabric glue or good quality PVA for general use and finishing the back of your hoop, double-sided tape for yarn-wrapping hoops, Mod Podge for collage and spray adhesive for fixing felt to the back of hoops.

**Iron and ironing board.** Always press your work as you go along. It gives a much smarter finish and is well worth the small amount of extra time it might take.

**Sewing machine (optional).** Most projects can be stitched by hand and even those that specify machine stitching can be adapted to work as hand-sewn ideas.

**Disposable nail file or sandpaper.** For smoothing rough hoop edges (often in the join below the screw) so they don't snag fabric.

**Washi or similar decorative tape.** For decorating hoops.

**Paint.** Acrylic paint is tough and easy to use, but tester pots of household emulsion also work.

**Wood stain.** Go for a medium shade, such as walnut or oak. Brush on a single coat for a light finish or add several layers to build up a darker colour.

**Small paintbrushes.** For applying paints, wood stain or glue.

**Crochet hook.** A 3mm–4mm (US D3–G6) size crochet hook will be needed.

**Computer and printer (optional).** For projects with a digital element.

# HOOP TREATMENTS

This section gives instructions on starting and finishing work with a hoop, plus descriptions of the hoop treatments used, including painting, staining, yarn wrapping, decorative tape, collage, crochet and braid.

**TOP TIP**

Stretch fabrics, such as jersey, are tricky to fix evenly across a hoop. For the best results, iron interfacing onto the back of the fabric to stabilize it before you start.

## Working with Hoops

All of the embroidery hoops used in this book are wooden because they are easy to source, simple to use and tend to hold fabric more securely than plastic hoops. They range in size from 7.5cm (3in) to 30cm (12in). When you're shopping for hoops, they'll usually be sized in inches, going up in increments of an inch at a time. Oval hoops are a little harder to find, but make a nice alternative or complement to their circular cousins.

### Starting

To fix fabric across your hoop, loosen the screw at the top edge just enough to accommodate the thickness of the fabric. Separate the inner and outer parts of the hoop, place the fabric on top of the inner hoop and then press the outer one down firmly on top. If there's too much resistance, loosen the screw a little more. Once the fabric is in place, you can gently pull at the edges to make any small adjustments. When it's smooth and taut in the hoop, use a screwdriver to re-tighten the screw.

### Finishing

Once your project is stitched and stretched into a decorated hoop, you need to finish off the back so it's neat and ready to display. There are various ways to do this, as follows. For an extra-neat finish, cut out a circle of felt and glue over the back of your hoop to cover all raw edges and knotted threads.

### Folding Over

This is the best option for lightweight or medium-weight fabrics. Trim the excess fabric from the edges of the hoop so you're left with just 1cm–2cm (³⁄₈in–³⁄₄in) all the way around. Spread glue over the back of the excess fabric and carefully press down against the inside edges of the hoop.

### Trimming Flat

This works best for thicker fabrics, such as wool or felt. Making sure your fabric is fixed very securely in place, trim the excess fabric flat against the back of the hoop.

### Gathering

This is a useful option if it's likely you'll need to remove the fabric from your hoop at any point, for instance to wash it. Trim the excess fabric, so it measures 4cm–5cm (1¹⁄₂in– 2in) all the way around. Fold over a 1cm (³⁄₈in) hem along the raw edge and secure with a gathering stitch. Pull the thread ends to gather the excess fabric and knot to secure.

**TOP TIP**

The fact you're choosing to display your work in an embroidery hoop doesn't necessarily mean you have to stitch it in a hoop. You can sew with it in a hoop or not, whichever you prefer for any given project.

# PAINTED HOOPS

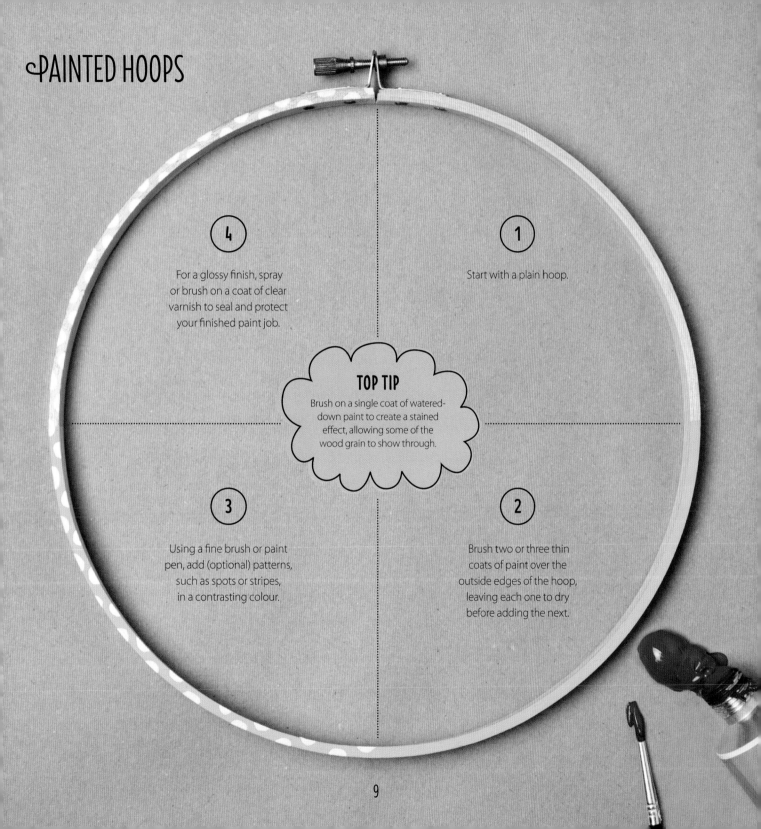

**4**

For a glossy finish, spray or brush on a coat of clear varnish to seal and protect your finished paint job.

**1**

Start with a plain hoop.

**TOP TIP**

Brush on a single coat of watered-down paint to create a stained effect, allowing some of the wood grain to show through.

**3**

Using a fine brush or paint pen, add (optional) patterns, such as spots or stripes, in a contrasting colour.

**2**

Brush two or three thin coats of paint over the outside edges of the hoop, leaving each one to dry before adding the next.

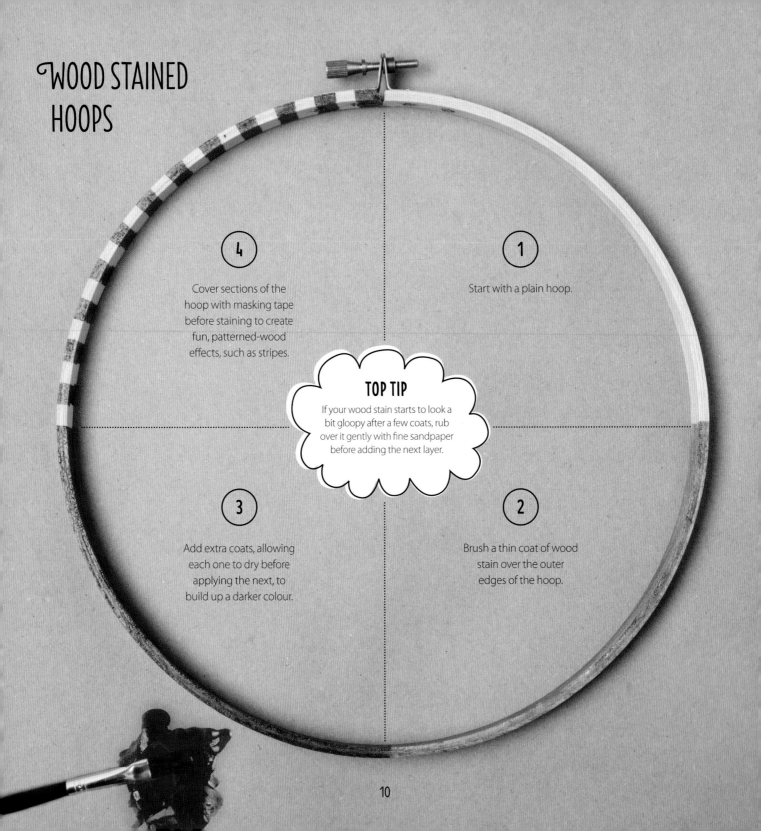

# WOOD STAINED HOOPS

**4**

Cover sections of the hoop with masking tape before staining to create fun, patterned-wood effects, such as stripes.

**1**

Start with a plain hoop.

**TOP TIP**

If your wood stain starts to look a bit gloopy after a few coats, rub over it gently with fine sandpaper before adding the next layer.

**3**

Add extra coats, allowing each one to dry before applying the next, to build up a darker colour.

**2**

Brush a thin coat of wood stain over the outer edges of the hoop.

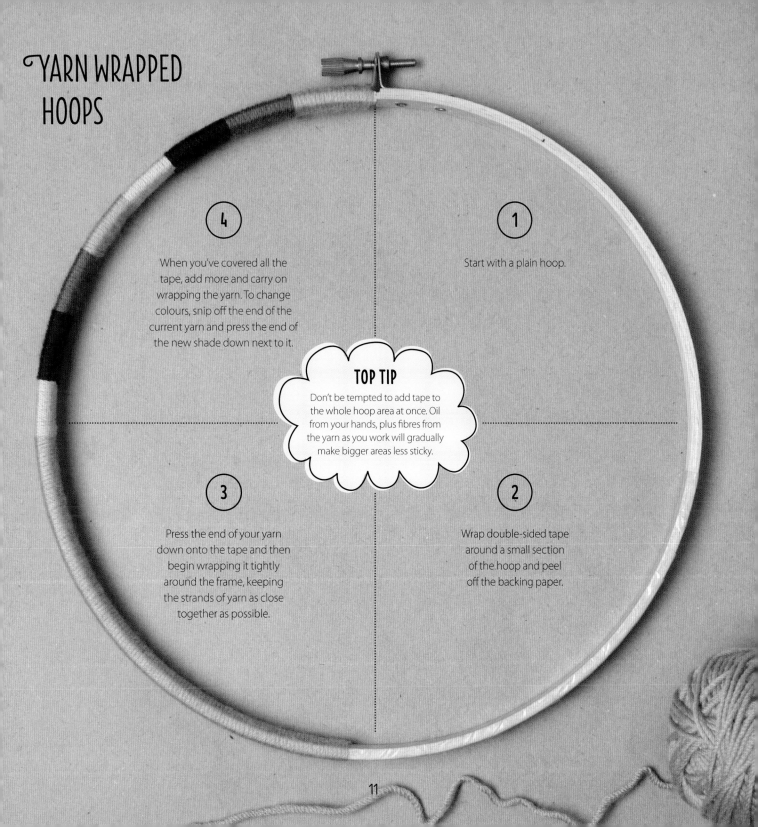

# YARN WRAPPED HOOPS

**4**

When you've covered all the tape, add more and carry on wrapping the yarn. To change colours, snip off the end of the current yarn and press the end of the new shade down next to it.

**1**

Start with a plain hoop.

**TOP TIP**

Don't be tempted to add tape to the whole hoop area at once. Oil from your hands, plus fibres from the yarn as you work will gradually make bigger areas less sticky.

**3**

Press the end of your yarn down onto the tape and then begin wrapping it tightly around the frame, keeping the strands of yarn as close together as possible.

**2**

Wrap double-sided tape around a small section of the hoop and peel off the backing paper.

# DECORATIVE TAPED HOOPS

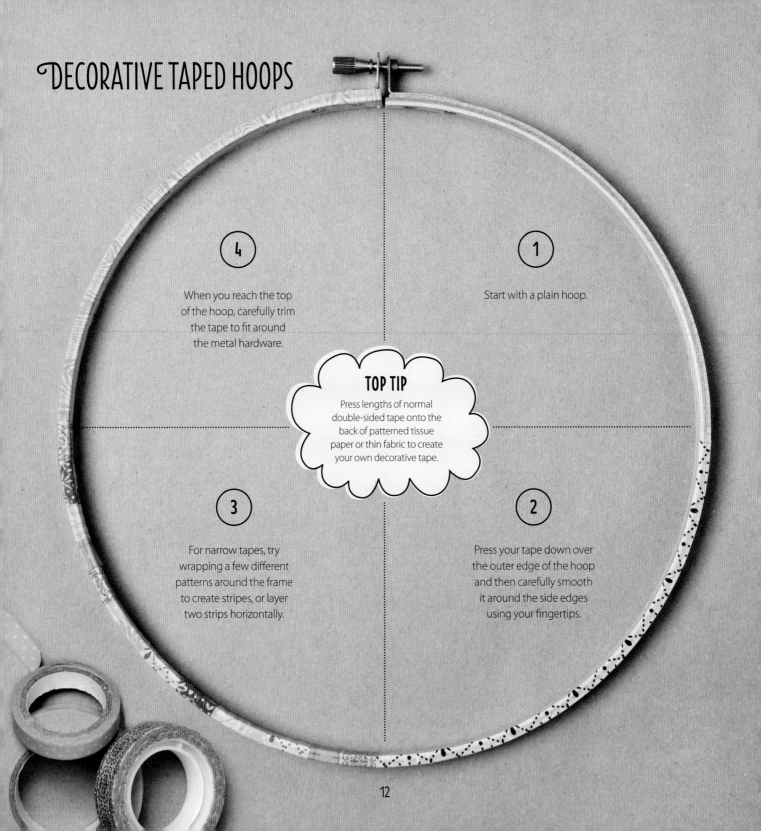

**4** When you reach the top of the hoop, carefully trim the tape to fit around the metal hardware.

**1** Start with a plain hoop.

### TOP TIP
Press lengths of normal double-sided tape onto the back of patterned tissue paper or thin fabric to create your own decorative tape.

**3** For narrow tapes, try wrapping a few different patterns around the frame to create stripes, or layer two strips horizontally.

**2** Press your tape down over the outer edge of the hoop and then carefully smooth it around the side edges using your fingertips.

# COLLAGED HOOPS

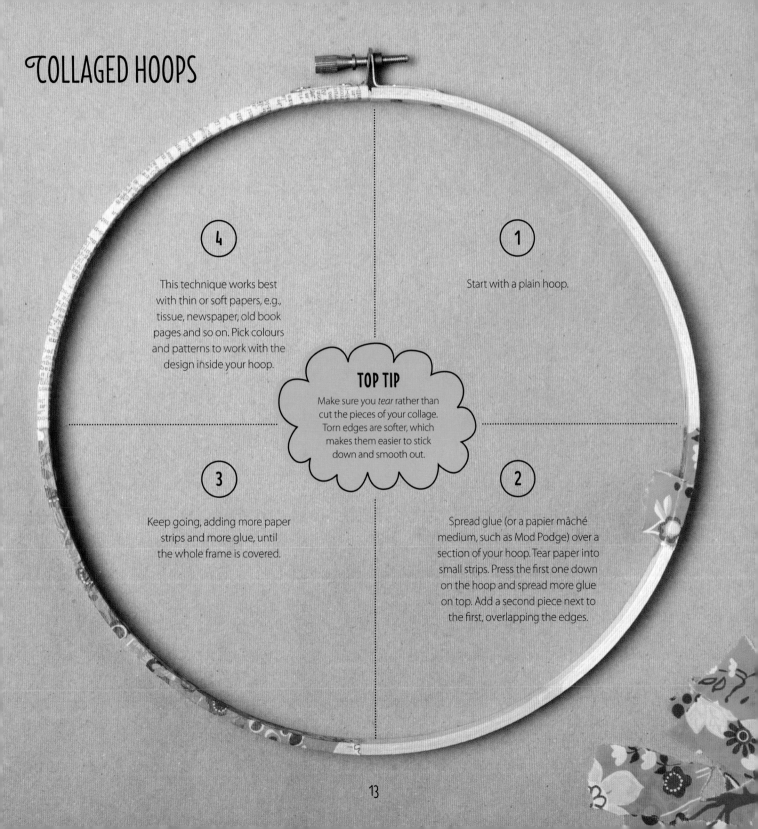

**4**

This technique works best with thin or soft papers, e.g., tissue, newspaper, old book pages and so on. Pick colours and patterns to work with the design inside your hoop.

**1**

Start with a plain hoop.

**TOP TIP**

Make sure you *tear* rather than cut the pieces of your collage. Torn edges are softer, which makes them easier to stick down and smooth out.

**3**

Keep going, adding more paper strips and more glue, until the whole frame is covered.

**2**

Spread glue (or a papier mâché medium, such as Mod Podge) over a section of your hoop. Tear paper into small strips. Press the first one down on the hoop and spread more glue on top. Add a second piece next to the first, overlapping the edges.

# CROCHETED HOOPS

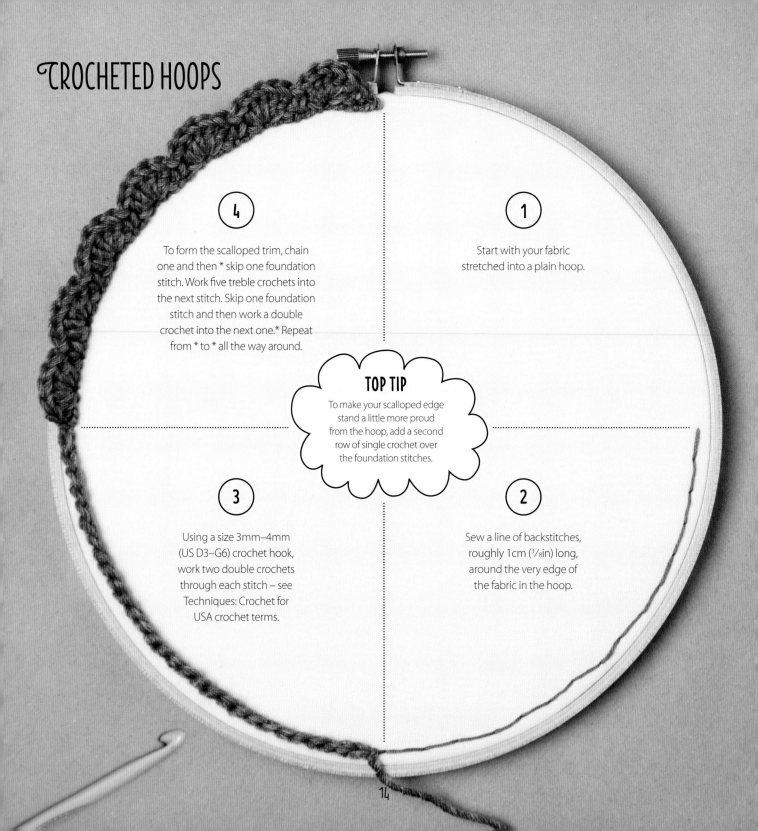

**4**

To form the scalloped trim, chain one and then * skip one foundation stitch. Work five treble crochets into the next stitch. Skip one foundation stitch and then work a double crochet into the next one.* Repeat from * to * all the way around.

**1**

Start with your fabric stretched into a plain hoop.

### TOP TIP

To make your scalloped edge stand a little more proud from the hoop, add a second row of single crochet over the foundation stitches.

**3**

Using a size 3mm–4mm (US D3–G6) crochet hook, work two double crochets through each stitch – see Techniques: Crochet for USA crochet terms.

**2**

Sew a line of backstitches, roughly 1cm (³⁄₈in) long, around the very edge of the fabric in the hoop.

# BRAIDED HOOP

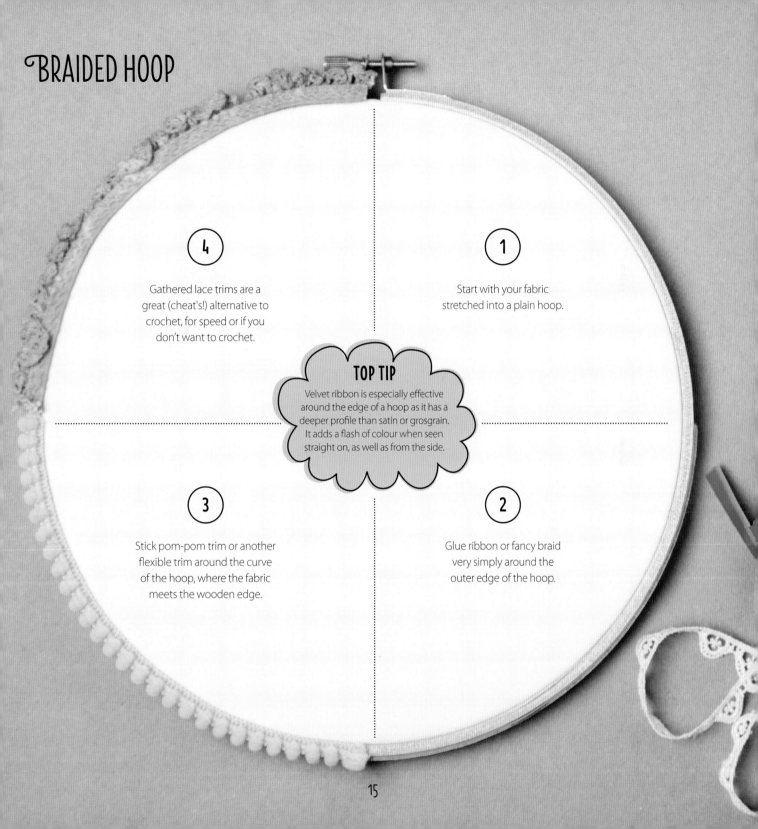

**4**

Gathered lace trims are a great (cheat's!) alternative to crochet, for speed or if you don't want to crochet.

**1**

Start with your fabric stretched into a plain hoop.

**TOP TIP**

Velvet ribbon is especially effective around the edge of a hoop as it has a deeper profile than satin or grosgrain. It adds a flash of colour when seen straight on, as well as from the side.

**3**

Stick pom-pom trim or another flexible trim around the curve of the hoop, where the fabric meets the wooden edge.

**2**

Glue ribbon or fancy braid very simply around the outer edge of the hoop.

# THE PROJECTS

## IN BLOOM

### YOU WILL NEED:

Embroidery hoop 18cm (7in)
Plain or patterned fabric
Faux flowers (e.g., silk,
crocheted, paper, fabric, metal,
flower-shaped buttons)

### TOP TIP

Sticking to a limited colour palette
– whether bold, pastel or neutral
shades – will help to unify the
different flowers and give your
bouquet a more cohesive look.

**1.** Decorate your hoop and stretch the fabric into place. Arrange the flowers in a group on top. Use a mixture of different types, sizes and materials, keeping them grouped together. Layer different flowers on top of each other, and add buttons or beads to make flower centres for some of them.

**2.** When you're happy with the arrangement, glue or stitch the flowers into place, one at a time.

# TOOTH FAIRY POCKETS

**1.** Copy the tooth template onto white fabric. Pin to a second layer of fabric and sew the two pieces together, leaving a small gap for turning. Trim away excess fabric and clip the seams to ease around the curved parts of the design. Turn out through the gap and stitch closed. Copy the eyes, nose and mouth and stitch into place.

**2.** Sew the tooth to your background fabric, slip stitching around the edges. Leave the top open, for slipping in lost teeth and fairy donations.

**3.** Fix double-sided tape around the edges of a plain or decorated hoop, leaving the top third free. Cut a 70cm (27in) length of ribbon and press one end down onto the sticky tape at the bottom edge of the hoop. Wrap the ribbon around the side of the hoop, pressing onto the tape as you go. Leave a loose section at the top to make a hanger and then wrap the ribbon around the other side of the hoop in the same way, lining up the ends so they meet at the bottom edge.

**TOP TIP**

Use the loop of ribbon to hang your tooth fairy pocket over a bedpost or door handle whenever it's needed.

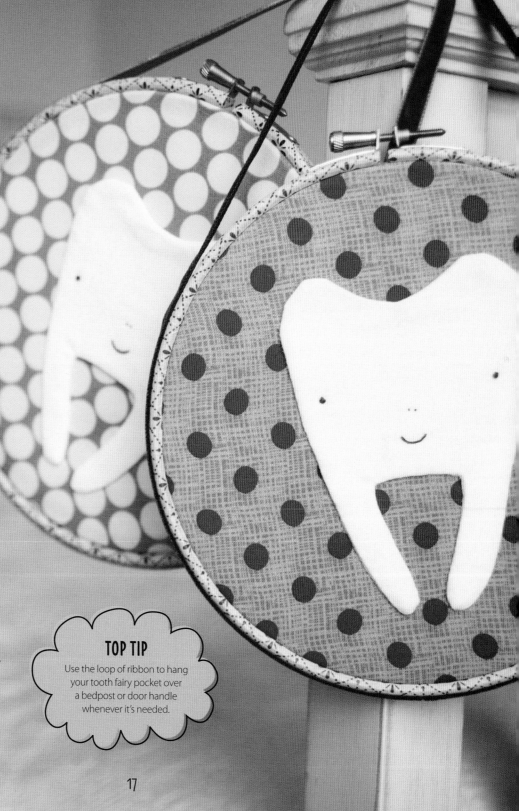

17

# BUTTONED UP

## YOU WILL NEED:

Embroidery hoop 18cm (7in)
Plain or lightly patterned fabric
Erasable fabric marker
Green and red buttons
Green and red
embroidery thread
Green and brown felt
Fabric glue or PVA

1. Trace the apple template onto your background fabric with an erasable fabric marker. Arrange buttons of different shapes and sizes inside the outline, filling as much of the space as possible. Stitch each one securely into position.

2. Copy the stalk and leaf shapes onto felt and cut out. Spread a thin layer of fabric glue onto the back of each piece and press into place at the top of the apple.

# PEAR-SHAPED

## YOU WILL NEED:

Embroidery hoop 15cm (6in)
Fusible web
Two contrasting patterned fabrics or one patterned and one plain
Green felt
Fine leather cord (brown) – faux is fine!

1. Trace the pear template onto fusible web. Iron onto the back of your fabric and cut out. Peel away the backing paper and iron into place on background fabric. Hand or machine stitch around the outer edges. Sew tiny, random straight stitches over one side of the pear to add extra detail and texture.

2. Cut out a leaf from green felt and sew at the top of the pear. Snip a short piece of leather cord and couch into place as a stalk.

### TOP TIP

This appliqué idea works with many silhouettes. Draw your own, search for free examples online or try it with other templates in this book.

# WHAT'S COOKING?

## YOU WILL NEED:

Embroidery hoops: 15cm (6in), 18cm (7in) and 13cm x 23cm (5in x 9in) oval

Plain and patterned fabrics

Erasable fabric marker

Fusible web

Sewing cotton or embroidery thread

## TOP TIP

These hoops would look fantastic in a dining room but you could hang them in the kitchen if you protect the hoop treatment with a coat of clear varnish (avoid crochet and yarn-wrapped edges).

**1.** Copy the template for each design directly onto the background fabric using an erasable marker.

**2.** Trace the appliqué sections of each template onto fusible web. Iron onto fabric, cut out and peel away the backing paper. Position the pieces over your outlined designs and iron into place. Sew around the edges of each appliquéd piece using backstitch and a single strand of sewing cotton or embroidery thread.

**3.** Add the outline and remaining details to each design, using backstitch and one strand of navy or black thread. If you use a gathering stitch on the back of the fabric rather than gluing it to the frame you'll be able to snip the gathering threads, remove the fabric, wash it and replace it in the hoop when required.

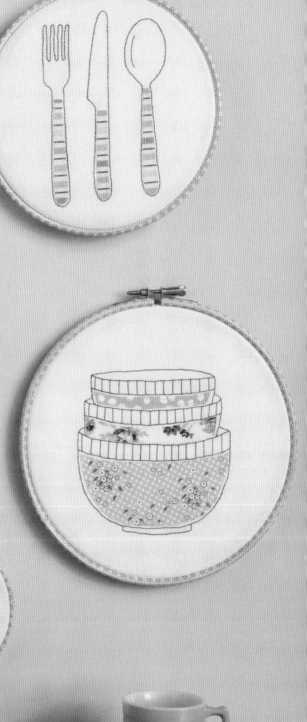

**TOP TIP**

The Velcro on the 'O' and 'X' buttons will stick to the surface of the felt, making this a perfect travel game. When you've finished playing, store the buttons in the bag, and hang it over the screw at the top of the frame to keep everything together.

## YOU WILL NEED:

Embroidery hoop 13cm (5in)

Felt

Erasable fabric marker

Embroidery thread

Ten flat buttons 2cm–2.5cm
(³⁄₄in–1in) in diameter

Scraps of fabric

PVA or fabric glue

Velcro spots

## FOR THE BAG:

Patterned fabric

Sewing thread

Button

Narrow ribbon

# NOUGHTS AND CROSSES

1. Stretch felt into the hoop and draw a simple grid pattern on top with an erasable fabric marker. Sew over the lines in a contrasting thread colour, using chain or split stitch.

2. Turn the hoop over and trim the excess felt flush with the back of the frame. Stick a circle of felt inside the recess to cover the back of the stitching.

3. Cut out a circle of fabric, roughly twice the diameter of one of your buttons. Sew a gathering stitch around the outside edge. Place the button in the centre, pull the thread ends so the fabric gathers around the button and knot the ends to secure.

4. Cut out an 'X' shape from felt and glue to the front of the covered button. Glue the hooked (scratchy) side of a Velcro dot to the back. Make nine more buttons in the same way, so you have a total of five with an X shape on the front and five with an O shape.

## To create the bag:

1. Cut two 9cm x 20cm (3¹⁄₂in x 8in) pieces of fabric. With right sides facing, sew them together around the edges, leaving a small gap at one side for turning through. Turn out, slip stitch the gap and iron for a neat finish.

2. Fold over 8cm (3¹⁄₄in) at one end of the rectangle. Sew a running stitch along each edge of the fold to create a small bag with a flap at the top. Sew a loop of thread at the end of the flap and a button in the centre of the bag to make a closure. Fix a length of ribbon to the back to make a hanging loop.

### TOP TIP

Use flat buttons with holes rather than the type with a shank. The method for covering them is the same as for self-cover buttons but the Velcro spot is used instead of a snap-on cover to hide the gathered fabric at the back.

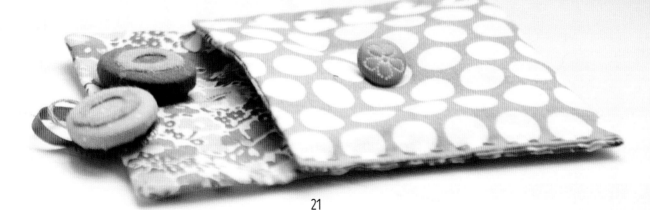

## TOP TIP

If you can't get chalkboard fabric, try painting normal fabric with several coats of blackboard paint. For the best results pick a fabric in a medium or heavy weight with a close weave.

# CHALK TALK

**YOU WILL NEED:**
Embroidery hoop 20cm (8in)
Chalkboard fabric
Coloured elastic

**1.** Decorate the hoop and then carefully stretch the chalkboard fabric into place. You'll probably need to loosen the screw quite substantially to begin with as the fabric isn't very flexible.

**2.** When it's firmly in place, trim away the excess fabric at the back. Cut a tiny strip of coloured elastic and fold under the ends. Stitch in place at one edge of the chalkboard, to make a loop for holding chalk.

# MAKING NOTES

**YOU WILL NEED:**
Embroidery hoop 18cm (7in)
Patterned fabric
Cork trivet (or cork tiles)
Craft knife
Felt

**1.** Decorate the hoop and stretch the fabric into place. Check that the trivet fits neatly into the recess at the back of the hoop; if not, trim to size with a craft knife.

**2.** Spread glue around the side edges of the trivet. Slip into place behind the fabric. Cut a circle of felt and glue across the back of the hoop.

## TOP TIP

Look out for fancy drawing pins to use with your pinboard.

# CROSS STITCH REPEATS

## To create the plaid design:

1. Stretch the Aida into your hoop and start sewing in the centre – see the Template section for the chart. Work the whole design, so it forms a diamond shape in the middle of the hoop.

## To create the chevron design:

1. Stretch the Aida into your hoop and draw a circle in the centre. Starting in the middle of the circle, begin working the cross stitch pattern in your first thread colour.

2. Stitch up to the edge of the outlined circle and then go back to the centre to finish off the first row, working up to the opposite edge of the circle.

3. Change thread colour and add the second chevron stripe next to the first one. Keep going, alternating between your chosen colours and stitching to the outlined edges of the circle, until you've filled the whole shape.

### TOP TIP

If you'd rather fill the whole hoop with either design, just keep repeating the pattern all the way out to the edges.

# SWEET HOME KEY RACK

## YOU WILL NEED:

Embroidery hoop 20cm (8in)
Plain fabric
Scraps of patterned fabric
Fusible web
Embroidery thread
Felt
Three cup hooks

**1.** Trace each template part separately onto fusible web. Iron onto the back of your patterned fabric and cut the pieces out neatly. Peel the backing paper and assemble the house on plain background fabric. Iron to fix into place.

**2.** Using one strand of embroidery thread, sew a fine outline around each piece. Use black for details on roof, door and windows, and white across the middle of the house.

**3.** Trace the frame outline from the template onto backing fabric and stitch over it with three strands of thread. Cut the heart from felt and glue in the centre.

**4.** Screw a cup hook into the bottom of the hoop, just below the heart. The pointed end should easily go through the wood and fabric as you twist it. Repeat with the other cup hooks, evenly spaced.

# SIMPLE TRANSFERS

### TOP TIP

Rub-ons come in a huge variety of designs. Try floral designs, spell out words with alphabet sheets or create a scene on a plain fabric background.

**1.** Iron the fabric and place face up on a hard surface (e.g., cutting mat or glass chopping board). Roughly cut out the rub-on and peel away the backing paper.

**2.** Position the rub-on over the fabric and use a lollipop stick or bone folder to rub firmly over the surface a couple of times. Carefully lift off the upper layer to reveal the transferred image.

**3.** Stretch the fabric into your decorated hoop and add any extra stitched details.

# POODLE DOODLE

**1.** Trace the poodle body template onto fusible web. Iron onto the back of your felt and cut out. Peel away the backing paper and iron on the background fabric. Trace the rest of the template (fluffy head, tail, legs and middle) directly on top.

**2.** Fill the outlined sections with French knots in shades of pink and red. Start with a single colour and sew the knots randomly over the first section. Continue, alternating between shades, and building up the knots so the shape is filled.

**3.** Finally, sew on the eye, using backstitch and add an extra French knot with black wool for a nose.

# DRESS-UP DOLL

## YOU WILL NEED:

Embroidery hoop 20cm (8in)

Plain or patterned fabric

Erasable fabric marker pen

Heavyweight interfacing

Embroidery thread

Pink marker pen

Patterned paper (e.g.,
scrapbooking papers)

Small, flat, circular magnets

White felt

Spray adhesive and PVA or fabric glue

Thin card

Embellishments (buttons,
ribbon, paper flowers)

1. Copy the doll template onto fabric using an erasable marker. Iron interfacing onto the reverse of the fabric. Start sewing over the marker lines. Use tiny satin stitches for the eyes, close-set lines of split stitch to fill in the boots, cross stitches to decorate the underwear and backstitch for everything else. Erase the marker-pen lines, and when the fabric is completely dry add two dots of pink ink for cheeks.

2. To make a hair bow, fold a scrap of paper in half and cut a triangle against the fold. Open out, and glue to one side of the doll's head, over her hair.

3. Turn the hoop over and place a small, round magnet behind the doll figure, positioning it near the top of her body, just below the neckline. Cut white felt to fit over the back of the fabric in the hoop and make a hole in the middle to accommodate the position of the magnet. Add a thin coat of

spray adhesive to one side of the felt and press into place on the back of the fabric.

4. Spread PVA or fabric glue over the back of two extra strips of felt, both about 6cm x 1.5cm (2$\frac{1}{2}$in x $\frac{5}{8}$in). Place them in an X shape over the back of the magnet, securing to the reverse of the hoop.

5. Copy the outline of each dress template onto thin card, and cut out. Copy and cut out again, this time from patterned paper and including extra details, such as pockets and collars. Assemble the patterned pieces on top of the plain background and glue together. Add buttons, ribbon or any extra embellishments.

6. Glue a magnet to the back of each dress, just below the neckline. To dress up your finished doll, place clothing over the figure so the magnet behind the fabric holds it neatly in place.

## TOP TIP

Adjust and adapt the clothing templates to suit your own style and tastes. Make them longer or shorter, add extra details and embellishments, or make them plainer – it's entirely up to you.

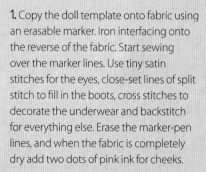

# CLIP A CORSAGE

1. Stretch the fabric into the decorated hoop.

2. Clip your corsage to the fabric, so it's beautifully displayed but can be easily removed when you want to wear it.

**YOU WILL NEED:**
Embroidery hoop 15cm (6in)
Patterned fabric
Corsage or large floral brooch

### TOP TIP
Pick a fabric with a bold or interesting design, so your hoop still looks good even when you take the corsage off.

# REDWORK

**YOU WILL NEED:**
Embroidery hoop 15cm (6in)
Plain or patterned fabric
Erasable fabric marker
Red embroidery thread

1. Trace the template directly onto fabric using an erasable marker.

2. Begin sewing, using two or three strands of red thread. Work the straight lines in a mixture of running stitch, backstitch and whipped backstitch. Use French knots for the marked dots and single (or detached) chain stitches for the leaves and central flower.

### TOP TIP
Using a lightly patterned fabric rather than the traditional white or cream gives a more contemporary look.

# VINTAGE TREASURES

## YOU WILL NEED:
Embroidery hoops: 15cm (6in) and 18cm (7in)
Vintage (or favourite) buttons, buckles and doilies
Coordinating fabrics

## To display buttons:

1. Arrange the buttons on your background fabric, either by colour, size, or in a more random order. Carefully stitch one button at a time into position.

## To display buckles:

1. Arrange buckles in a similar way to buttons. Don't be afraid to mix sizes, placing some vertically and other horizontally. Add one or two stitches to the bar of each buckle to hold in place, and then go back and add extra stitches to secure more firmly.

## To display doilies:

1. Place the top part of your embroidery hoop over a piece of fabric and arrange the doilies on top, so that you can see how they'll look when framed. Sew them into place with tiny, stitches around the edges and across the centre of each doily. Stretch the fabric into your hoop. You can either trim away excess around the edges, or, to keep the doilies intact, fold it over and fix to the back with double-sided tape.

### TOP TIP
Gather together some of your favourite vintage finds or collections of found objects and display them in a group of hoops.

29

# RETRO RABBIT

1. Trace the rabbit template onto fusible web. Iron onto the back of your fabric and cut out. Peel the backing paper away from the left ear *only* – snip it off at the base of the ear, so just that section of web is exposed.

2. Place the ear on top of another piece of the same fabric, with wrong sides facing. Iron to fix the two pieces together. Cut around the outside edge, so you have a double layer of fabric making the ear.

3. Peel off the rest of the backing paper and iron the rabbit on to your background fabric. Fold over the top part of the left ear and press, so it flops forwards. Sew around the outside edge of the rabbit (excluding left ear), using backstitch and a single strand of thread.

4. Sew a white button to the head for the eye. Cut a circle of black felt to fit over the centre of the button and glue into place. Make a tiny white pom-pom and sew on as a tail.

## TOP TIP

If you're struggling to make a small enough pom-pom for the tail, cheat! Make the smallest one you can, then snip all round with scissors – giving it an all-over haircut.

# LACECAPS

## YOU WILL NEED:

Embroidery hoop 18cm (7in)
Plain and patterned fabrics
Fusible web
Light brown felt

1. Cut a piece of fabric, roughly 23cm (9in) square, and sew a second, smaller piece across the bottom edge.

2. Copy the mushroom templates onto fusible web and iron onto felt or fabric, as marked. Cut out and peel away the backing paper. Assemble the pieces on the background and iron into place.

3. Sew around the colourful cap of each mushroom using backstitch. Add single straight stitches to the base of the two smaller mushrooms for gills. Use small groups of satin stitches, worked across the full width of the felt, to create the stripy effect at the top of each stalk.

# RE: DESIGN

## YOU WILL NEED:

Embroidery hoop 18cm (7in)
Selection of patterned fabrics
Linen or other plain background fabric
Fusible web
Embroidery thread

1. Select motifs from the patterned fabrics and cut them out roughly. Iron fusible web onto the back of each piece and then cut more precisely around the detail or motif you want to use. Arrange the pieces on a plain background and, when happy with the design, iron to fix into position.

2. Stitch around the edges and details of the various pieces to highlight and hold them more securely in place.

## TOP TIP

It's a good idea to cut out more motifs or images than you think you'll need so you can play around with the design and see which work best together.

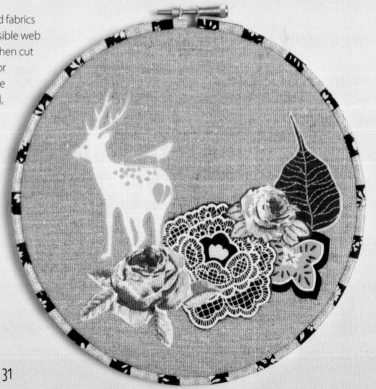

31

# MIX TAPE SCREENPRINTS

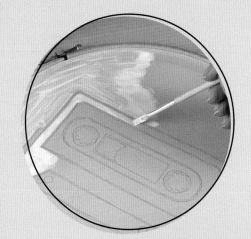

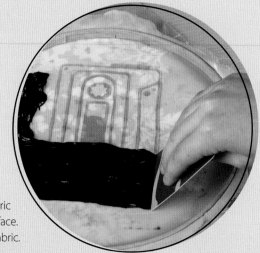

**1.** Stretch voile or sheer fabric into the larger hoop and trim away excess at the edges. Trace the cassette template onto the fabric in pencil.

**2.** Using a small brush, fill in all the negative space (white areas on the template) with Mod Podge. Apply it fairly thickly, as though you were painting, out to the edges of the hoop frame (see picture detail 1). Leave to dry and then brush on a second coat in the same way.

**3.** When the screen is completely dry, press your chosen fabric to remove any creases and place it on a flat, wipe-clean surface. Place the screen on top, so the voile is directly against the fabric.

**4.** Mix equal parts of paint and screen-printing medium in a small container. Add several blobs to your screen, just above the cassette image, and stretching along the width. Hold the screen firmly in place with one hand. With the other hand, use the plastic card to spread the paint mixture across the image (picture 2). Go over the whole image two or three times, making sure you keep the screen still.

**5.** Very carefully lift the screen away from your fabric. (It helps to have a friend hold the fabric down at this point.) Hang the printed fabric up to dry. Wash your screen straight away if you plan to use it again. Mount the design in the hoop.

## TOP TIP
Screen-printing medium slows down the drying time of acrylic paint, helps prevent clogging and screens can be washed more easily after use. If you don't plan on re-using a screen, just use acrylic paint on its own.

# FEATHER BUTTERFLIES

1. Decorate your hoop and stretch the fabric into place. Place the butterflies on top, moving them around until you're happy with the way they look.

2. Glue each butterfly into position, or if they have soft bodies, sew them to the fabric background with two or three single stitches through the centre of each one.

### TOP TIP

Handmade butterflies, punched or die-cut from multiple layers of paper would make a pretty alternative to the feather kind, and are just as easy to glue or sew into place.

# STITCHED SILHOUETTE

1. Trace the ampersand template onto counted-thread fabric using an erasable pen. Stretch the fabric across the hoop. Starting at one edge, fill in the shape with cross stitches – see the Template section for the chart. Sew right up to the edges, going just over the outline when it falls in the middle of a stitch.

2. To make stripes, sew several rows in your first colour and then switch to the next. You can make all stripes the same width, or vary the number of rows in each one.

### TOP TIP

As an alternative, try stitching in a single colour rather than stripes.

# GRANNY CIRCLE

## YOU WILL NEED:
Embroidery hoop 15cm (6in)
Wool or yarn in five different colours
Crochet hook 3.5mm (US size E/4)
Plain or patterned fabric
Coordinating embroidery threads

**1.** Crochet a granny circle, following the pattern on this page – see also Techniques: Crochet for USA crochet terms.

**2.** Stretch your fabric into the hoop. Pin the granny circle in the centre. Stitch it into place, removing the pins as you go, and using tiny stitches in colours to match each shade of yarn.

## ROUND 1

Ch4 and join with a slip stitch to make a circle.

Ch3, then 1tr into the circle.

*Ch1, 2tr into the circle*

Repeat from * to * 5 times.

Ch 1, then slip stitch into the top of the first 3ch you made.

## ROUND 2 (CHANGE COLOUR)

Attach yarn to one of the spaces.
Ch3, then 1 tr, into the same space.
Ch1, 2tr into the same space.

*Ch1, 2tr into the next space, ch1 and 2tr into the same space.*

Repeat from * to * 5 times.

Ch1, then slip stitch to join to top of the first 3ch you made.

## ROUND 3 (CHANGE COLOUR)

Attach yarn to one of the spaces.
Ch3, then 2tr, into the same space.

*Ch1, 3tr into the next space.*

Repeat from * to * 11 times.

Ch1, then slip stitch to join to top of the first 3ch you made.

## ROUND 4 (CHANGE COLOUR)

Attach yarn to one of the spaces.
Ch3, then 2tr, into the same space.

*Ch1, 3tr into the next space.*

Repeat from * to * 11 times.

Ch1, then slip stitch to join to top of the first 3ch you made.

## ROUND 5 (CHANGE COLOUR)

Attach yarn to one of the spaces.
Ch3, then 6tr, into the same space.

* Ch1, 7 tr into the next space.*

Repeat from * to * 11 times.

Ch1, then slip stitch to join to top of the first 3ch you made.

35

# UP AND AWAY

## YOU WILL NEED:

Embroidery hoop 13 x
23cm (5 x 9in) oval
Patterned fabrics
Cardboard
Natural linen or hessian fabric
Daisy trim or other
decorative braid

1. Copy the balloon centre template onto your fabric and cut out. Fold over and pin a narrow hem along each edge.

2. Place the balloon centre on your background fabric and re-pin to hold it in place. Stitch the two pieces together, either with invisible hemming stitches or using a bolder running stitch in a contrasting thread colour. Remove the pins and press. Stretch the fabric into your decorated hoop.

3. Cut two pieces of cardboard 4.5cm x 5cm (1³⁄₄in x 2in) and two pieces of linen or hessian 6.5cm x 7cm (2⁵⁄₈in x 2³⁄₄in). Take the first piece of cardboard, spread glue over one side and press down firmly onto one of the linen rectangles. Fold the edges of the linen over onto the back of the cardboard and glue in place. Repeat to cover the second piece of card with linen. Set aside to dry.

4. Cut two 30cm (12in) lengths of thread. Use a needle to take the first one down through the fabric in your hoop, just next to the centre panel, and then back up on the opposite side. Do the same with the second piece of thread, but 3cm–4cm (1¹⁄₄in–1⁵⁄₈in) further up the side of the hoop.

5. Pull the thread ends so they hang evenly at either side. Fix double-sided tape to the back of your first cardboard rectangle. Press the thread onto the tape, so the balloon basket hangs evenly and at the right height.

6. Snip off excess thread. Press the second piece of linen card on top, so the threads are sandwiched between. Glue on daisy trim to decorate the basket front.

## TOP TIP

Snip off the corners of your linen rectangles before you fold the side edges over onto the back to reduce bulk and give a smoother finish.

# MY ONLY SUNSHINE

**TOP TIP**

You can use any paper for raindrops. Try gift wrap or scrapbooking paper, old books, maps or the patterns inside envelopes. Magazines and catalogues are great – look out for clothing or homeware with interesting patterns.

## To create the clouds:

**1.** Trace the cloud templates onto fusible web. Iron the large one onto white felt and the smaller one onto grey fabric or felt. Cut out and peel away the backing paper. Pin on the background fabric with the white cloud overlapping the grey one. Do not iron yet.

**2.** Fold a piece of paper in half and cut out a raindrop shape through both layers. Glue the raindrops together, back to back, with the end of a 12cm (4¾in) length of thread sandwiched between them. Make ten to twelve raindrops this way.

**3.** Thread one of the raindrop pieces onto a needle. Un-pin the bottom edge of the white cloud and lift up slightly. Sew the thread end to the background fabric beneath the cloud. Repeat with the other raindrops, arranging as desired.

**4.** Remove the pins from both clouds and iron to fuse. Sew a line of small running stitches around the edge of each one. Mount the design in your decorated hoop.

## To create the sun:

**1.** Stretch your fabric into the decorated hoop. Sew a line of orange running stitches around the outside edge. Add a second row of stitches in a lighter shade, off-setting them. Add more rows in progressively lighter shades ending with cream or off-white.

# MULTI-HOOP ZOO

## YOU WILL NEED:
Fusible web
Plain and patterned fabric
Embroidery threads

### FOR THE DOG:
Two embroidery hoops 18cm (7in)
Black felt

### FOR THE GIRAFFE:
Three embroidery hoops each 15cm (6in)
Wool or yarn (yellow and orange)

## To create the dog:

**1.** Use the template provided and trace the front and back body sections of the dog onto fusible web. Iron onto plain fabric, cut out and then iron onto separate pieces of background fabric.

**2.** Stretch each fabric piece into a hoop, and stitch around the edges by hand or machine.

**3.** Copy the ear template onto contrasting fabric and cut out twice. With right sides facing, sew the pieces together around the edges, leaving a small gap at one edge. Turn the fabric right way out through the gap and then sew up the gap.

**4.** Sew the top of the ear to the top of the head, catching the stitches around the seam so they appear invisible. Finish off by stitching on a sleepy eye and sticking a circle of black felt into place as a nose.

## To create the giraffe:

**1.** Use the template provided and trace the giraffe head, neck and body sections onto fusible web. Iron onto patterned fabric, cut out and then iron each one onto a separate piece of background fabric.

**2.** Stitch around the edges of the giraffe by hand or machine, or a combination for a fun look.

**3.** Thread yellow wool down through the fabric near the top of the head and back up a short distance away, leaving two short tails. Secure each of these flat with embroidery thread, using tightly spaced couching stitches to make the horns. Snip off the yarn, leaving a short end to splay out at the top of each one.

**4.** Sew loops of orange thread or wool down the back of the head and neck. Stitch the eye into place.

**5.** For the tail, thread two pieces of yellow wool down through the fabric at the back of the body, and then back up a few millimetres away. Pull the four ends so they're roughly even in length and plait together. Knot a piece of thread around them to secure and then unravel the rest to give the tail a fluffy end.

**TOP TIP**

To stretch the dog across three hoops just add an extra straight section in the middle. Or, try adding two extra sections to make a four-hoop version, and hang them so the dog wraps around a corner on a wall.

# WRAP PARTY

## YOU WILL NEED:

Embroidery hoop 20cm (8in)
Patterned fabric
Double-sided adhesive tape
Embroidery threads

## TOP TIP

Remove the hoop screw while you add the tape and fabric. It's easier to access the top edges if you don't have to tuck strips beneath the screw.

**1.** Cut patterned fabric into strips 1cm–2cm ($^3$/$_8$in–$^3$/$_4$in) wide, and as long as you can make them (anything over 50cm/20in is perfect). Set the inner hoop aside and wind double-sided tape around the outer hoop, starting as close to the screw as possible. Aim to cover roughly a quarter of the hoop in tape. Peel away the paper backing as you go.

**2.** Take a fabric strip and press the end down onto the tape. Begin winding the fabric around the tape-covered hoop as tightly as you can. Add more tape once you've covered the first section. When you come to the end of a fabric strip, press the end of a new one into place and carry on wrapping. Keep going until the whole hoop is covered, and then cut off any excess fabric.

**3.** Stretch fabric into the wrapped hoop. Decorate with stitching to highlight details.

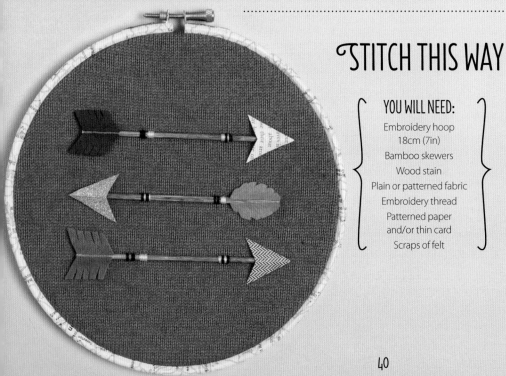

# STITCH THIS WAY

## YOU WILL NEED:

Embroidery hoop
18cm (7in)
Bamboo skewers
Wood stain
Plain or patterned fabric
Embroidery thread
Patterned paper and/or thin card
Scraps of felt

**1.** Use sharp scissors to cut three bamboo skewers 10cm (4in) long. Brush each with a thin coat of wood stain. Allow to dry and place all three on the background fabric, spacing out evenly. Add a few stitches at either end to decorate and hold in place.

**2.** Use the template to cut arrow heads from patterned paper or thin card. Fold in half and glue one to each bamboo. Snip three pairs of arrow ends from coloured felt (see templates). Stick one to each of the sticks to finish.

## TOP TIP

Make a collaged hoop frame from pieces of an old map to tie in with your arrow-themed design.

# PETITE PINCUSHION

## YOU WILL NEED:

Embroidery hoop 10cm (4in)
Jersey or other stretch fabric
Small drinking glass
Crushed walnut shells (or
sawdust, coarse sand or rice)
Thick cardboard
Felt
Ribbon, lace or braid

**1.** Stretch the fabric evenly in the hoop but don't tighten the screw. Place on top of a small glass and gently push downwards so the fabric stretches and looks baggy above the hoop. Tighten the screw to secure.

**2.** Working from the back, pour crushed walnut shells (or alternative) into the fabric so it fills out and forms a dome shape. Glue a circle of thick card over the back of the hoop to seal the filling inside.

**3.** Decorate the hoop and cover the card circle with a coordinating piece of felt.

# FRAMED PATCHWORK

## YOU WILL NEED:

Embroidery hoop 23cm (9in)
Small pieces of plain
and patterned fabric
Buttons (optional)

**1.** Sew strips of fabric together to make a square of patchwork about 5cm (2in) larger all round than the diameter of your hoop. Iron the patchwork flat and then stretch it across the hoop, as you would with a plain piece of fabric.

**2.** Finish off by stitching on buttons to decorate (or an embroidered detail, such as a name).

## TOP TIP

This project is perfect for displaying small pieces of your favourite fabrics. Save up scraps as you sew, or gather from a single source, e.g., children's old clothes.

# HEADS UP

## YOU WILL NEED:

Embroidery hoop 20cm (8in)
Plain fabric
Erasable fabric marker pen
Embroidery thread
Coloured felt
Fusible web
Permanent pink marker pen

**TOP TIP**

Try mixing and matching different faces and hairstyles to customize your finished hoop. You could create a set to look like your family, friends, or the characters from a favourite book or TV show.

1. Copy the head templates onto plain fabric using an erasable marker. Stitch over the eyes, nose, mouth and lower part of each face using one or two strands of embroidery thread.

2. Trace the hair, hat and moustache templates onto fusible web, iron onto felt and cut out. Peel away the paper backing and iron each piece into place over the relevant head.

3. Sew around the edges of the felt hair to secure. Add a line of stitches over each moustache. Add extra lines of white stitching over the hat to create stripes, and decorate buns or pigtails with bundles of French knots.

4. Wash away any remaining marker lines and when the fabric is completely dry add dots of pink ink for cheeks on each face.

# LITTLE RED

## YOU WILL NEED:

Embroidery hoops 20cm
(8in) and 15cm (6in)
Aqua wool or felt
Indigo cotton fabric
Fusible web
Felt (light brown, grey, red, white,
black and flesh-toned)
Embroidery thread
Thin white card

## To create Little Red:

**1.** Cut aqua wool or felt large enough to stretch across your hoop. Use fusible web to stick a wide strip of indigo fabric on top.

**2.** Cut narrow strips of light brown felt to make tree trunks. Arrange over the background and fix in place with random straight stitches, working in from the side edges towards the centre.

**3.** Trace the Little Red templates onto fusible web, iron onto felt and fabric, as marked, and cut out. Assemble the pieces on your background and iron into place. Stitch around the edges of the cape and tie thread into a bow at the neck.

**4.** Use one strand of embroidery thread to sew on the face and knees. Work satin stitches in black and red over the lower legs for boots and socks.

## To create the wolf:

**1.** Cut a light brown tree trunk and stitch it to the indigo background fabric, as before.

**2.** Trace the wolf templates onto fusible web, iron onto felt, and cut out. Copy and cut out the teeth from white card. Assemble the pieces on your background and iron into place. Use short, straight stitches all over to secure and look like fur.

# BRUSH STROKES

**YOU WILL NEED:**

Embroidery hoops 13cm (5in),
15cm (6in) and/or 18cm (7in)
Photoshop, or other imaging software
Digital brushes
Printer paper
Spray adhesive
Plain and/or patterned fabric
Inkjet printer

**1.** Use digital brushes to create a design in Photoshop, or similar software. Try a single large shape to fill your hoop, or use several brushes in a mixture of sizes to build up a pattern. For the smallest of the hoops here, a single brush was stamped in white onto a dark blue background. The design on the medium-sized hoop was built up using lots of different brushes in a single colour and then printed onto patterned fabric. The design on the largest hoop was made in a similar way, using a variety of brushes, stamped in black on a white background. The image was then flattened and the space between the brushes filled with a contrasting colour.

**2.** Once the design is ready, iron your fabric to remove any creases. Coat a sheet of normal printer paper with spray adhesive. Press down onto the back of your fabric and then trim any excess from around the edges.

**3.** Print your digital image directly onto the fabric, running it through the printer as you normally would a piece of card or photo paper. Allow the ink to dry for a few minutes and then peel the fabric away from the paper and stretch across a decorated hoop.

**TOP TIP**

You can buy inkjet fabric sheets or make your own. To do this, spray temporary adhesive onto a sheet of printer paper, and press a well-ironed piece of plain cotton fabric down on top. Trim the edges so that paper and fabric are the same size, then run through your printer as usual. Allow the ink to dry for a few minutes before peeling the fabric away from the backing paper.

**TOP TIP**

Digital brushes can also be used as embroidery patterns. Print out on plain paper and trace onto your fabric, or print directly onto fabric and stitch over the printed outlines to add extra detail and texture.

# WITH LOVE

## YOU WILL NEED:

Embroidery hoop 15cm (6in)
Alphabet stamps
Black ink
Plain or patterned fabric
Chipboard (particle board) letters

1. Paint your hoop a light colour and leave to dry. Apply a small amount of ink to the first of your stamps and press down gently onto the side edge of the hoop. Repeat with a second stamp and then keep going, working your way all round the hoop.

2. When the ink is dry, stretch the fabric into the hoop. Decorate with chipboard letters, glued into place.

### TOP TIP

'O' and 'X' stand for hugs and kisses (of course!), but you could spell out a word or phrase with your stamps, or use symbols (e.g., a flower or heart shape) to build up a design.

# AHOY SHIPMATES!

## YOU WILL NEED:

Embroidery hoop 20cm (8in)
Fusible web
Scraps of patterned fabric
Felt (red and white)
Embroidery threads

1. Trace the boat templates onto fusible web. Iron each one onto the back of a different piece of fabric and cut out. Peel away the backing paper and assemble all pieces on your background fabric, except the small felt portholes. Iron into place.

2. Machine stitch around the outer edges of each piece, using thread to match the fabric. Use two lines of stitching, keeping them close to the fabric edges. Try using a darning or zipper foot to see exactly where you're stitching.

3. Sew four or five lines of brown stitching between the flag and top of the boat for the pole. Iron the portholes into position and add a cross stitch in the centre of each.

# BUTTON GARDEN

## YOU WILL NEED:

Embroidery hoop
15cm (6in)
Blue and green fabrics
(plain or patterned)
Buttons in a variety
of shapes and sizes
Green embroidery thread

1. Cut a piece of blue fabric large enough to fill your hoop and then sew a narrower strip of green along the bottom edge. Arrange buttons across the upper half of the hoop, mixing up colours, shapes and sizes and sew each one into place.

2. Sew a single line of running or split stitches underneath each button to create a flower stem. Use open chain stitches to add simple leaves, either along the stalk or just beneath the button flower itself.

**TOP TIP**

Fix tiny paper flowers behind a few of the buttons for added texture and variety.

# PHOTO FINISHED

## YOU WILL NEED:

Embroidery hoop 15cm (6in)
Inkjet printer
Inkjet fabric sheets or paper
and fabric to make your
own (see Top Tip with the
Brush Strokes project)
Embroidery thread
Fabric scraps
Buttons, beads, flowers
for embellishments

1. Print your chosen photograph onto inkjet fabric and stretch into an embroidery hoop.

2. Add extra details or highlight existing features with fabric, thread, beads or buttons. Try using fancy stitches to add pattern to plain areas, making a tie or skirt from patterned fabric, or fixing beads over pieces of jewellery.

**TOP TIP**

Adjust the techniques and supplies you use so they complement the subject of the photograph.

# SIMPLE STENCILS

## To create the whale:

**1.** Cut freezer paper roughly the same size as the fabric. Trace the whale template in the centre of the paper. Cut out, leaving the rest of the paper intact to form a stencil.

**2.** Place the stencil on top of the fabric and iron. The freezer paper will adhere temporarily to the fabric. Punch a tiny circle from leftover freezer paper and iron in place to make the eye.

**3.** Apply paint to the fabric through the stencil. Use a brush with firm bristles and work with a pouncing motion, rather than brushing the paint on. Set aside to dry. Peel the stencil (and eye) away from the fabric.

## To create the anchor:

**1.** Trace the anchor template onto freezer paper. Cut out and paint, as before. When dry, use a contrasting colour to stamp dots onto the shape through the stencil. Allow the dots to overlap the paper edges in places. Leave to dry and then peel off the stencil.

### TOP TIP

For a different effect, try reverse stencilling. Iron the cut-out (positive) shape onto the fabric and paint around the outside of the fabric instead.

48

# TO THE LIGHTHOUSE

## YOU WILL NEED:

Embroidery hoop 20cm (8in)

Plain or patterned fabrics
for sea, sky and grass

Navy-and-white striped fabric

Light-coloured cotton or linen

Felt (red and black)

Fusible web

Embroidery threads

### TOP TIP

The lighthouse was made using an old T-shirt, which is a great alternative to buying fabric by the metre/yard if you only need a small amount, or can't find what you want.

1. Transfer the template pieces onto fusible web, iron on to felt or fabric, as marked and cut out. Construct the scene on blue background fabric and iron into place.

2. Copy the scallop pattern onto the sea and embroider using curved lines of white and turquoise backstitch. Sew around the edges of the other pieces, adding a grid pattern to the top of the lighthouse and straight stitches for balcony railings. Add a few wide V shapes for seagulls.

# FLOCK TOGETHER

## YOU WILL NEED:

Embroidery hoop 18cm (7in)

Flocking powder or ultra-fine Flower Soft™

Plain fabric

Selection of ribbon and braid

### TOP TIP

Loose flock is a soft, powdery substance that can be applied in a similar way to glitter, creating a velvety or felt-like texture.

1. Working on the side and front edges of the hoop, spread glue over a small section at a time. Sprinkle flocking powder on top and shake off the excess. Repeat this until the whole frame is covered. Set aside to dry. Add a second layer of flock in the same way.

2. Arrange strips of ribbon and braid on plain background fabric. Once you're happy with the design, glue or stitch each piece into place before stretching the fabric into your flocked hoop.

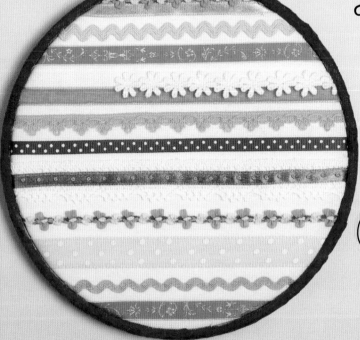

49

# HERE COMES THE SUN

**YOU WILL NEED:**

Embroidery hoops (various)

Sun-print fabric (cyanotype)

Items to make your prints
(see suggestions after
project instructions)

Tray or hardback book

Glass (e.g., borrowed
from a picture frame)

1. Working indoors in a dimly lit space (e.g., room with doors and curtains closed), cut a piece of sun-print fabric large enough to stretch into your hoop. Lay the fabric on a flat, mobile surface, such as a tray or hardback book, and place your chosen object(s) on top (see detail picture 1). Add a piece of glass on top to stop lighter items from moving around or blowing away. Heavier pieces, such as keys, will be fine on their own.

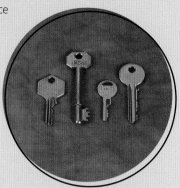

2. Take the whole thing outdoors and place it in direct sunlight. Make sure there's nothing nearby to cast even a faint shadow on the fabric. Leave it to expose for the recommended length of time.

3. Bring the fabric back indoors once it's fully exposed. Lift the items off and immediately rinse the fabric in cold water (picture 2). You'll see the chemicals washing off (they're usually a greenish colour) but the water should quickly run clear. Once this happens, squeeze out the excess and set the fabric aside. It will gradually become darker as it dries and the impression will become clearer.

4. Press your finished print to remove any creases and then stretch into a decorated hoop. Display a variety of sun-printed pieces together for even greater impact.

## TOP TIP

It's best to make your prints around midday when the sun is at its highest. As well as being faster this also cuts down the likelihood of non-flat items (e.g., keys) casting shadows, which would blur the edges of your print.

### PRINT KNOW-HOW

Sun printing (also known as cyanotype, or blueprinting) relies on light from the sun to expose an image on chemically treated fabric. The amount of time this takes can vary hugely depending on the weather, the time of day and time of year. For instance, even on a bright day, the weaker winter sun will take longer to expose your image than it does on a hazy day in midsummer. When you're ready to make your prints, cut a few small sample pieces of fabric and expose them for different lengths of time to work out exactly how long the process will take on that particular day.

### WHAT TO PRINT?

Any solid object you place on the cyanotype fabric will leave an impression. Generally, the flatter the object, the sharper the image will be. Try some of these ideas.

Leaves and grasses

Feathers

Cut-out paper shapes

Doilies (paper or fabric)

Pieces of lace

Coins

Buttons

Keys

Alphabet letters (e.g., fridge magnets)

Safety pins

Paper clips

Scissors

Jewellery

Old photo negatives

Designs drawn on clear plastic with a heavy black marker pen

# CREWEL INTENTIONS

## YOU WILL NEED:

Embroidery hoop 20cm (8in)
Plain linen fabric
Erasable fabric marker
Crewel or tapestry wools

**1.** Copy the flower templates onto your fabric using an erasable marker. Working with green wool, sew along both flower stems using split stitch.

**2.** Fill in the leaves with satin stitch, working from outer edges towards the centre line. Use coloured wool and satin stitch to fill in each flower head (see picture detail). Work white French knots to finish off the details.

**3.** Cut two strips of contrasting fabric and iron fusible web onto the back of each. Peel away the backing and iron into place just below the flower stems. Add two or three rows of stitching (hand or machine), across the centre to secure.

## SATIN STITCH

When sewing satin stitches around a curved shape fan out your stitches, so they're closer together on the inside edges than on the outside. Try not to overlap them or let them drift apart so the fabric is seen. Work some guide stitches around the shape first. Space them out fairly evenly, and then go back and fill in the gaps. This makes it easier to judge the angle of your satin stitches and helps you fan them out more evenly.

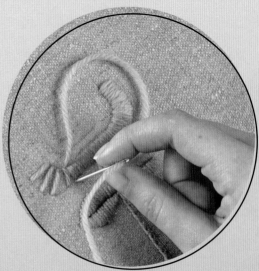

# MEMORY KEEPERS

**YOU WILL NEED:**

Embroidery hoops: 18cm
(7in) and 20cm (8in)
Old or outgrown items of clothing

1. Choose your mementoes. As well as preserving children's clothes, such as a special dress that's too small for your daughter or a little boy's favourite outgrown sweater, you can also save pieces of your own clothing. Any item that is worn out but just too special to throw away is fair game! Even if you don't have children of your own, offering to preserve something like this for a friend would be a lovely gesture and a unique gift.

2. Take the item of clothing you want to preserve and select the area that would look best framed and displayed. You could pick a particular detail, such as the smocking on a dress or fancy pocket on a shirt, or just highlight part of the pattern or design.

3. Stretch the fabric into your decorated hoop. Trim or fold over any excess around the edges.

### TOP TIP

To preserve part of a stretchy item, iron interfacing onto the back of the material first. This will help to keep the fabric steady as you fix it into the hoop.

# ꙅPRING MOBILE

1. Separate the hoops and discard the outer part of each one. Decorate both hoops as desired.

2. Layer the flowers, buttons and feathers, and stitch through the centre of each layer. Glue into place on either side of the larger hoop.

3. To make the bird, cut out the template pieces from felt and fabric. Snip into the edges of the feathers (as marked on the template), and sew the two beak pieces together around the edges. Sew one wing to each body piece using a plain running stitch. Sew a sleepy eye onto each piece.

4. Pin the fabric gusset between the two red marks on one of the bird pieces, with right sides facing, and stitch together along one side of the gusset. Add the second bird body to the other side of the gusset in the same way.

5. With right sides facing, pin and then stitch the bird body pieces together, catching the beak at the front and the tail feathers at the back. Leave a small gap just below the tail for turning through. Turn the bird the right way out and press. Push stuffing in through the gap and then slip stitch it closed. Fix the finished bird to the small hoop using a couple of stitches underneath.

6. Cut a long length of invisible thread and fold it in half. Tie the centre around the top of the small hoop. Make another knot roughly 2.5cm (1in) above the first one. Take the two sides of the thread around the top of the larger hoop and knot again. Use the remaining length of thread to hang your finished mobile.

## TOP TIP

Feeling lazy? Perch a store-bought bird on your mobile instead!

## TOP TIP

Don't throw away the outer part of each hoop – use the pieces to make a second mobile instead. Perch the bird on the screw mechanism of the smaller one and stick a flower over it on the outer hoop.

# TYPEWRITTEN

**YOU WILL NEED:**

Embroidery hoop 18cm (7in)

Fusible web

Plain and patterned fabrics (including white to make the 'paper' part of the design)

Felt (dark grey and light grey)

White embroidery thread

**1.** Trace the template pieces onto fusible web. Iron each one onto the back of felt or fabric and cut out. Peel away the backing paper, assemble the pieces on the background and iron in place.

**2.** Machine stitch around the outer edges of each piece, using white on the 'paper' and black or dark grey for the rest. Sew two lines of stitching close to the fabric edges.

**3.** Copy, then stitch, a handle at the left side of the typewriter. Sew two rows of eight to ten white French knots as typewriter keys over the grey felt keyboard at the front.

# VINYL LOVE

**YOU WILL NEED:**

Embroidery hoop 18cm (7in)

Black fabric

White pastel or chalk pencil

Fusible web

Patterned fabric

**1.** Cut a piece of fabric, roughly 25cm (10in) square. Place the outer part of your hoop on top and draw around it using white pastel or chalk pencil. Draw a second circle, roughly 8cm (3in) diameter in the centre. Machine stitch around the outer circle with black thread, and slowly spiral in towards the edge of the inner circle.

**2.** Draw a 6cm (2¼in) circle onto fusible web and iron onto the back of a piece of patterned fabric. Cut out, remove the paper backing and iron the circle in the centre of the black fabric. Stitch around the edges to secure. Stretch the finished record into a black-painted hoop.

# HIM AND HER

## YOU WILL NEED:

Embroidery hoop 15cm (6in)
Flesh-toned paint and fabric
Embroidery thread
Scraps of pink fabric
Felt
Old pair of spectacle frames (optional)
Fabric hair bow (optional)

1. Paint your hoop(s) to match your fabric colour and allow to dry. Copy the face template onto fabric and stretch into the hoop.

2. Add the eyes, mouth and nose in backstitch, and satin stitch for the pupils. Cut two circles of plain or patterned pink fabric and stitch into place for cheeks.

3. To make the boy's hair: Copy the boy hair templates onto felt and cut out. Glue the side pieces into place along the edges of the hoop. Stitch along the dotted lines, working in about 5cm (2in)

from each edge towards the centre. Glue the edges to the hoop and finish stitching the rest of the lines, working through the felt and the background fabric to secure the centre sections.

4. To make the girl's hair: Copy the girl hair templates onto felt and cut out. Stitch along the dotted lines on the back and side sections and then glue into place over the hoop. Finish the front piece as for the boy's hair.

5. Glue the boy's glasses and the girl's hair bow into place to finish.

## TOP TIP

Customize your faces by using different hair or skin colours, adding freckles, beards, moustaches or different hairstyles.

# BEGINNER'S GEOMETRY

## YOU WILL NEED:
Embroidery hoop 18cm (7in)
Plain or patterned fabric
Erasable fabric marker
Black embroidery thread

1. Copy the template or draw a freehand version onto fabric. Stretch the fabric into your decorated hoop.

2. Using two strands of embroidery thread, sew a long stitch over each of the lines, working around the design until you've covered them all.

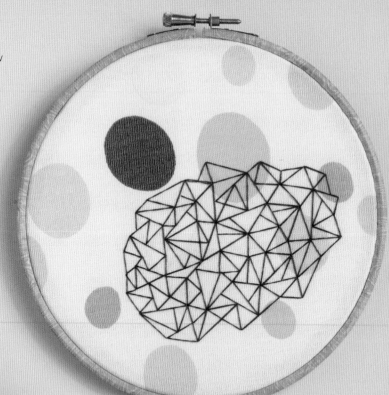

# DANDY LION

## YOU WILL NEED:
Embroidery hoop 18cm (7in)
Erasable fabric marker
Yellow fabric
Small scraps of pink fabric
Dark grey felt
Dark grey, white, yellow and pink embroidery thread

1. Transfer the eyes, mouth, nose and whiskers from the template onto yellow fabric. Copy the cheeks onto pink fabric and the tip of the nose onto dark grey felt. Cut out the pieces and sew into place.

2. Stitch the eyes, mouth and nose using dark grey embroidery thread. Make French knots in white for the whiskers and sew random yellow straight stitches inside the nose area to add extra texture.

# QUILTY PLEASURES

## YOU WILL NEED:

Embroidery hoop 18cm (7in)
Cotton wadding (batting)
Cheater cloth (see Top Tip)
Embroidery thread

**1.** Place the inner section of your hoop on top of two layers of wadding and draw around the inside. Cut out, snipping through both waddings to make a double-layered circle.

**2.** Cut cheater cloth roughly 25cm (10in) square. Place on top of the wadding circles and pin the three layers together.

**3.** Starting in the centre, sew around the edges of the fabric squares. Use small running stitches through all layers and stitch around all squares that are over (or overlap) the wadding circles.

**4.** Don't stretch the fabric into the hoop until you've finished stitching. Leaving it a little looser as you work will help to emphasize the quilted effect and give your finished project a tactile, padded texture. Stretch the work into the hoop – the wadding circles should fit neatly into the recess at the back. Trim or neaten the top layer of fabric as normal.

## TOP TIP

Using 'cheater cloth' can save much time. This fabric looks like patchwork but is actually a printed design, usually made up of squares in a variety of patterns and colours.

# MAN-BROIDERY

{
### YOU WILL NEED:

Embroidery hoops: 23cm (9in),
15cm (6in) and 13cm (5in)
Patterned fabric (four different prints)
Sewing thread
Fusible web
Plain, flesh-toned fabric
Black, grey and red felt
Embroidery thread
Erasable fabric marker
}

## To create the star:

1. Trace the star template onto fusible web and iron onto patterned fabric. Cut out, peel off the backing paper and iron onto a small piece of knitted fabric (e.g., a piece from an old sweater). Iron interfacing onto the back of the fabric before stretching it into your hoop.

## To create the moustache:

1. Trace the moustache template onto fusible web and iron onto dark grey or black felt. Cut out, peel off the backing paper and iron onto striped fabric. Sew around the edges using small, straight stitches to secure.

## To create the strongman:

1. Cut two rectangles of fabric, one 20cm x 30cm (8in x 12in) and the other 10cm x 30cm (4in x 12in). With right sides facing, sew them together at one long edge and press the seam flat.

2. Trace each piece of the strongman template separately onto fusible web. Iron onto the back of the fabric or felt and cut the pieces out neatly. Peel away the backing paper and assemble the figure on your background. Iron to fix into place.

3. Stretch the fabric into your hoop. Using a single strand of dark grey embroidery thread, stitch a fine outline around the head, body, clothes and dumb-bells. Use straight stitches to hold the felt hair, moustache, bar and stars in place.

4. Draw on the eyes, eyebrows, nose and mouth with an erasable fabric marker and then stitch over them with black thread. Add a sprinkling of small straight stitches over the body to make some manly chest hair.

### TOP TIP
The two smaller hoops essentially use the same idea – a plain felt shape on a patterned background, or vice versa. The fusible web holds the shape in place well enough to display your hoop, so it's up to you whether to add stitching around the edge or not.

# JEWELLERY HANG-UPS

## YOU WILL NEED:

Embroidery hoops: 18cm
(7in) and/or 13cm x
23cm (5in x 9in) oval
Medium to large shank buttons
Plain or patterned fabric
Sticky foam pads, about
3mm ($\frac{1}{8}$in) square
Embroidery thread

**1.** Stretch fabric into your decorated hoop and arrange the buttons on top. You can use finished buttons, self-cover buttons or a mixture. Ensure there's room for a necklace to hang freely from each one by placing the buttons in a straight line, or staggering at different heights with space below.

**2.** Take the buttons off one at a time, marking their place. Fix three sticky foam pads to each button – one on either side and one near to the bottom edge. The foam pads will help to stabilize the buttons.

**3.** Peel the backing off each pad and press the button back into place on the fabric. Use embroidery thread to stitch each button into place.

## TOP TIP

Self-cover buttons are easy to use. You only need a tiny amount of fabric so they're great for using up scraps. To make your project even more personal, embroider a tiny detail or design onto the fabric first.

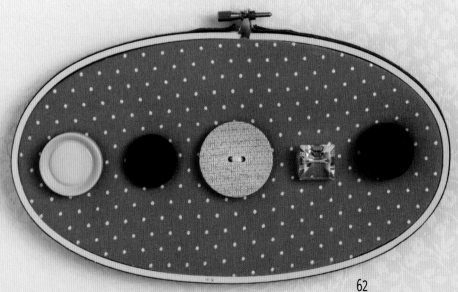

# GLITTER CHANDELIER

**1.** Working on the side and front edges of your embroidery hoop, spread glue over a small section at a time. Sprinkle glitter on top and shake off the excess. Continue adding more glue and glitter until the whole frame is covered. Set aside to dry.

**2.** Add a second layer of glitter in the same way. When the glue is completely dry, spray on a coat of clear varnish to stop the glitter shedding.

**3.** Trace the chandelier template onto the fabric. Stitch over the main outline using black thread, by hand or sewing machine. Add white candles and yellow flames.

**4.** Sew lines of beads on each tier of the chandelier and then add two rows of backstitch in silver thread.

# HOWEVER YOU SLICE IT

## YOU WILL NEED:

Embroidery hoops 18cm (7in)
and/or 20cm (8in)
Patterned and plain fabrics (red,
yellow and a dough-like colour)
Fusible web
A compass (for drawing circles)
Felt (dark red, light red, coral, green, black,
russet, cream light brown, white and purple)
Embroidery threads

## To create the pizza:

1. Paint the hoop frame the same dough-like colour as your background fabric and set aside to dry. Draw two circles 19cm (7½in) and 17cm (6¾in) in diameter onto fusible web. Iron the larger one onto red fabric and the smaller onto yellow fabric. Cut both out and then iron the yellow circle on top of the red one.

2. Cut the double-layered circle into six equal segments. Iron on to your background fabric, allowing very narrow gaps between the 'slices'. Machine stitch around the edges to secure.

3. Copy the topping templates onto fusible web, iron onto felt and cut out. Arrange on the pizza background, and iron into position. Use embroidery threads to hand sew around the edges to secure and decorate.

## To create the fruit slices:

1. To make an orange or lemon slice, draw a circle slightly smaller than your hoop onto plain paper. Fold it into eighths and then unfold and cut out one of the sections, snipping just inside the fold lines and curving all three points.

2. Use this as a template to cut out eight orange or yellow pieces of fabric. Arrange them on an off-white background, again allowing small gaps between the segments, and stitch into position.

# SUPER HERO

## YOU WILL NEED:

Embroidery hoop 18cm (7in)
Digital patterned paper
Photoshop, or other imaging software
Scanner and inkjet printer
Printer paper
Plain and patterned fabrics
Spray adhesive
Embroidery thread
Fusible web
Black or dark grey felt
Wooden or chipboard letter 'S'

**1.** Open the digital patterned paper file and check it is sized to fit into your hoop. Copy just the outline of the cat template and then scan. Place it on top of the patterned paper and select the area inside the outline. Switch to the patterned paper layer and press delete. The outlined image should now be blank, or white, on your screen. Delete the layer with the original scanned cat image.

**2.** Print the file onto fabric, following the instructions in steps 2 and 3 of the Brush Strokes project.

**3.** Add the details from the cat template to your printed fabric using faint pencil lines. Stitch around the outline of the cat and over the pencil lines using black or dark grey thread.

**4.** Copy the mask and T-shirt templates onto fusible web, iron on to felt and fabric respectively and then cut out and press into place. Finish off by gluing an 's' for 'super' to the front of the shirt.

## TOP TIP

Don't use erasable marker pen on the printed fabric unless you're certain your printer inks are waterproof. For the same reason, turn off the steam when ironing the fabric.

# SHE LOVES ME KNOT

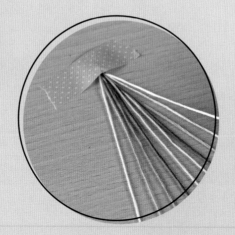

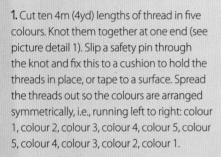

1. Cut ten 4m (4yd) lengths of thread in five colours. Knot them together at one end (see picture detail 1). Slip a safety pin through the knot and fix this to a cushion to hold the threads in place, or tape to a surface. Spread the threads out so the colours are arranged symmetrically, i.e., running left to right: colour 1, colour 2, colour 3, colour 4, colour 5, colour 5, colour 4, colour 3, colour 2, colour 1.

2. To start knotting, take the thread on the far left-hand side (colour 1) and knot it twice around the thread next to it (colour 2). Slide the knots as far up the thread as they'll go.

3. Knot the same thread (colour 1) twice around the next length of thread (colour 3), and then twice around the next one again (colour 4). Your original strand (colour 1) should end up in the middle.

4. Repeat steps 2 and 3, using the thread from the far right-hand side. When this is finished, the two threads that started on the outer edges (both colour 1) should be side by side in the centre. Knot them together twice.

5. Keep knotting from the outside edges in, repeating steps 3 to 5. Your band will start to take shape, with the coloured threads forming a chevron pattern along the length (picture 2). When the band is long enough to go around the edge of your hoop, stop knotting.

6. Spread a good amount of PVA glue over the both ends of the band – just below the starting knot and just ahead of the last rows you knotted. Cover a section roughly 1cm (³⁄₈in) wide at each end and allow the glue to soak through all of the threads. When completely dry, make a straight cut across the centre of each glued section; the adhesive should give you two secure, slightly stiffened ends.

7. Spread glue around the edges of your hoop and press the band down firmly on top. Use clothes pegs to hold it in place as the glue dries.

8. Stretch fabric across the decorated hoop. Cut out a selection of heart shapes from felt and glue to the fabric, either in a neat row or randomly over the surface.

## TOP TIP
Use yarn instead of embroidery thread for a chunkier band. You can also try other friendship bracelet patterns, as long as they're narrow enough to sit comfortably around the edge of a hoop.

**TOP TIP**

The threads for this project are much longer than those you'd use to make a wrist friendship band. To avoid tangling, wrap them around a thread-holder or scrap of card before you start knotting.

# PAPER PLANE

## YOU WILL NEED:

Embroidery hoop 18cm (7in)

White acrylic paint

Saucer or palette

Pencil with an unused
eraser at the end

Plain fabric

Black embroidery thread

### TOP TIP

Use a new pencil, so the circular
eraser has crisp edges. Practise
stamping on scrap fabric first
to get the hang of how much
pressure you need to apply to
get the best impression.

1. Spread a little white acrylic paint onto a saucer or palette. Dip the eraser end of a pencil into the paint and press it down onto the fabric. Repeat, to build up a pattern of dots. Set aside to dry.

2. Copy the paper plane template onto the spot-printed fabric. Sew along the trail part using running stitch and go over the plane with backstitch.

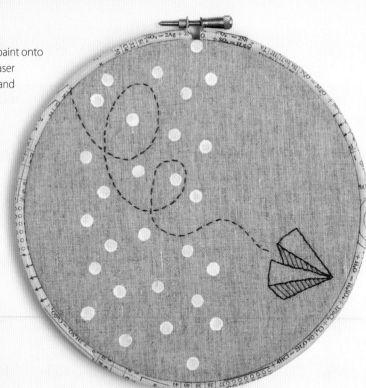

# HIPSTER RABBITS

## YOU WILL NEED:

Embroidery hoop 18cm (7in)

Digital picture or photograph

T-shirt transfer paper

Plain or patterned fabric

### TOP TIP

The transferred image will be reversed
when you iron it on to your fabric.
If your chosen image would look
wrong in reverse (e.g., if it includes
text), reverse it on screen before
printing on the transfer paper.

1. Select a picture or photograph and re-size to fit your hoop in Photoshop or other imaging software. Print out onto T-shirt transfer paper.

2. Following the instructions on the packaging, iron the transfer onto plain or lightly patterned fabric (bear in mind patterns will usually show through the transferred image). Stretch the fabric into your decorated hoop.

# MEGA STITCHING

**YOU WILL NEED:**

Embroidery hoops 30cm
(12in) and/or 10cm (4in)
Plain or counted-thread fabric
Erasable fabric marker
Embroidery threads

## To create the big star:

**1.** Enlarge the cross stitch chart in the Template section to fit your large hoop. Instead of working on counted-thread fabric, trace the stitches as a pattern of crosses directly onto plain fabric, using an erasable marker. Sew over each X with the full six strands of embroidery thread.

## To create the small star:

**1.** Use the chart at actual size and stitch onto Aida or similar counted-thread fabric.

# PHOTO PORTRAITS

## YOU WILL NEED:

Embroidery hoop 20cm (8in)
Head and shoulders
photograph of subject
Computer and printer
Fusible web
Plain and patterned fabrics
Erasable fabric marker
Embroidery threads

**1.** Find (or take) a photograph where the subject is facing the camera. Using photo software or an online photo editor, convert the image to grayscale and then add a sketch filter or effect (see picture detail 1). Print out the image at a size that fits comfortably into your hoop.

**2.** Trace over the image to create a simple, stylized drawing. Include the outline of the face, eyes, ears, nose, mouth and hair (picture 2). Add the neck and shoulders (including clothing). Make small adjustments as you go along so the drawing looks clear and simple.

**3.** Trace the hair and clothing pieces onto fusible web and iron onto the back of your chosen fabrics. Cut out and then peel away the backing.

## TOP TIP

The filter or effect you use on your photograph will vary depending on the software. It may be called 'sketch', 'charcoal', 'photocopy' or something else, but will ideally enhance the details and edges of your image, so it looks more like a drawing.

70

**4.** Trace the rest of the image onto the background fabric using an erasable marker. Position the hair and clothing on top and iron to fix in place (picture 3).

**5.** Sew over the outline and details of the face using backstitch and two or three strands of embroidery thread. Fill in the eyes with satin stitch. Use more backstitch to outline and add any extra details to the clothing. Instead of sewing around the edges of the hair, fill the area with short, random straight stitches to add extra texture. Lastly, iron a scrap of fusible web onto the back of some pink or red fabric. Cut out two small circles for cheeks. Iron into place and then sew.

### TOP TIP

Photoshop (or Elements) is great if you have it, but if not there are plenty of free online photo editors that work just as well for a project like this. Try picmonkey.com, lunapic.com, gimp.org or just search for 'online photo editing'.

# PATCHED HEXAGONS

## YOU WILL NEED:
Embroidery hoop 20cm (8in)
Thin card
Lightweight patterned fabrics
Erasable fabric marker
Plain cotton or linen fabric
(for the background)
Embroidery thread

**1.** Use the template to cut a hexagon from thin card. Draw around this onto your first piece of fabric and cut out. Fold over and press a narrow hem along each edge. Make ten to twelve hexagons this way.

**2.** Pin the hemmed hexagons to the background fabric and stitch in place around the edges using tiny running stitches. Use the template to trace some hexagons onto the background fabric and stitch just inside the outline of each one.

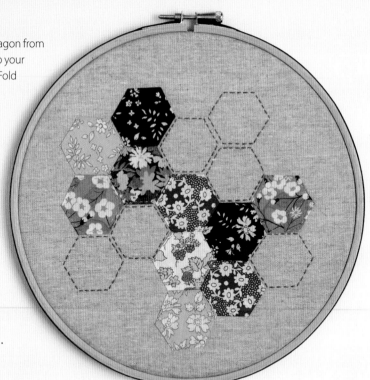

# FRAME A DETAIL

## YOU WILL NEED:
Embroidery hoops: 7.5cm
(3in) and 10cm (4in)
Novelty or bold-patterned fabric

**1.** Pick fabric with a particular detail or motif you'd like to highlight. Centre the detail in your hoop *before* you cut it to size.

**2.** Once you're happy with the way it's framed, stretch into position and tighten the screw. Frame larger details on their own, or make a group of several smaller ones and display together.

### TOP TIP
Novelty fabrics often include details that are perfect for framing. With braid or trim to decorate the edges, it's also a great gift idea.

# PICK POCKETS

## YOU WILL NEED:

Embroidery hoop 23cm (9in)
Plain and patterned fabrics
Fusible interfacing

### TOP TIP

You can space the stitching lines for your pockets evenly or at varying distances apart, depending on what you want each pocket to hold.

**1.** Cut a piece of fabric roughly 28cm (11in) square from background fabric, and a smaller piece 28cm x 12.5cm (11in x 5in) from the pocket fabric. Iron interfacing onto the back of the pocket piece.

**2.** Cut out a 3cm (1¼in) wide strip of contrasting fabric. With right sides facing, sew this to the upper edge of the pocket fabric. Press the seam flat and fold over a narrow hem along the opposite edge of the contrasting strip. Fold the strip over the top of the pocket fabric and stitch the hemmed edge to the seam.

**3.** Pin the pocket fabric to the background, lining up the bottom and side edges. Sew vertical lines from top to bottom of the pocket fabric, going through all layers. Stitch one line to make two pockets, two lines to make three pockets, and so on.

**4.** Finally, decorate your hoop. With the pocket section at the bottom, stretch the fabric into place. It's simple to adjust the sizes if you want to add pockets to a larger or smaller hoop. Cut the background fabric roughly 5cm (2in) larger than the hoop size, and make the pockets just under half the height.

# PLAY AND DISPLAY

## YOU WILL NEED:

Embroidery hoop 20cm (8in)
Fine string or thread
Scraps of fabric
Mini clothes pegs

**1.** Decorate the inner and outer hoops separately. Cut 30cm (12in) of string. Wrap one end around the inner hoop, a third of the way down from the top. Knot on the outside edge to secure. Stretch across the hoop and wrap around, keeping the string taut. Knot and trim any excess. Repeat with another string, two-thirds of the way down.

**2.** Re-join the inner and outer hoops and tighten the screw. Fold and stick small strips of fabric in half over the string, cutting the ends into a V to make tiny flags. Fill the gaps between with notes and photos, suspended on tiny clothes pegs.

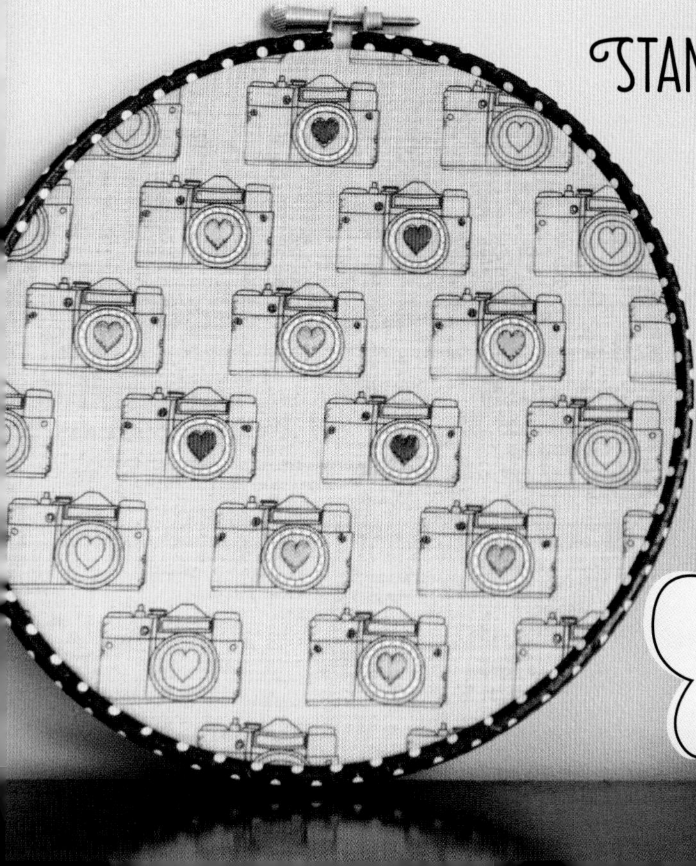

# STAMP AND STITCH

## YOU WILL NEED:

Embroidery hoop 18cm (7in)
Clear stamp and acrylic block or rubber stamp
Black pigment or dye-based ink pad
Embroidery threads

**1.** Tap the ink pad onto your stamp and press down firmly onto fabric to make your impression. Repeat to build up a pattern, either at regular intervals or randomly, all over the background.

**2.** When the ink is dry, stitch over selected details on some of the stamped impressions. Fill in small areas (like the hearts) with satin stitch, outline other parts with backstitch and add French knots to highlight.

## TOP TIP

To build up a regular pattern, place graph paper over a light box and tape your fabric on top. Use the squares to keep the gaps between each stamped impression even and equal in size.

# MISS MIXED-MEDIA

## YOU WILL NEED:

Embroidery hoop 18cm (7in)
Patterned fabric
Acrylic paint (white
and flesh-toned)
Small paintbrush
Dark blue felt
Scraps of white or cream fabric
Erasable fabric marker
Embroidery thread
Pink permanent marker
Paper flowers

1. Trace the template outline onto your fabric in pencil (not erasable marker or any kind of water-soluble ink). Fill it in using a small brush and white acrylic paint and allow to dry. Brush on two coats of flesh-toned paint over the top, making sure each one is dry before adding the next.

2. Copy the cap and swimsuit templates onto fabric and felt, respectively. Cut both out and stitch the swimsuit into place over the figure. Cut two strips of white or cream fabric and glue on top to decorate. Glue the cap into place.

3. Draw features onto the painted face, this time using an erasable marker. Stitch over them using two or three strands of embroidery thread. Remove any remaining ink lines with a damp cloth. When the face is completely dry, draw on pink cheeks with a permanent marker.

4. Finally, glue on a row of paper flowers to decorate the front of the cap.

## TOP TIP

If you need to iron the fabric after painting, place it between some tea towels and press gently, without steam. You should be able to remove creases without affecting the dry paint.

# FLOWER SWAP

## YOU WILL NEED:

Embroidery hoops 20cm (8in)
and/or 13cm x 23cm (5in x 9in)
Plain or patterned fabrics
Erasable fabric marker
Paper, silk or handmade flowers
Pom-pom maker or thick
cardboard (optional)
Yarn (optional)
Florist wire (optional)

## POM-POM DIY

**1.** Draw a 3cm (1¼in) circle inside a 5cm (2in) circle, forming a doughnut shape. Cut out and repeat to make a second doughnut.

**2.** Hold the two pieces of card together and start wrapping wool around the ring. Cover the card and carrying on wrapping until the hole in the centre has almost disappeared.

**3.** Push the point of your scissors down through the wool towards the centre. Keeping the point between the two layers of card, carefully cut the wrapped wool around the edges. Slip a length of yarn between the two layers of card, wrap it all the way around securing the wool bundle, and tie in a firm knot.

**4.** Pull the rings out and roll the finished pom-pom between your hands to fluff it into shape.

## To create the vase:

**1.** Cut a single piece of fabric to make your background, or join two different pieces together for a more eclectic look. Copy the vase template onto fabric using an erasable marker. Pin to a second piece of fabric with right sides facing. Sew together along the marker pen outline, leaving a small gap for turning. Trim away excess fabric and cut across corners to remove bulk. Turn through the gap and sew closed.

**2.** Position the vase on your background and slip stitch around the side and bottom edges to fix into place. Finish off by slipping a flower or two into the vase – either handmade or bought.

## To create the flowers:

**1.** You could use a pom-pom maker (they're inexpensive and quicker than the DIY option) or create your own flowers using scraps of card (see below). Make two, and then fold a 30cm (12in) length of wire in half. Push each end into one of the pom-poms, adding a small amount of glue to hold in place.

### TOP TIP

Have fun changing the blooms in your vase every season – try tulips in spring, faux-roses in summer, seed pods for autumn and silk poinsettias or a sprig of mistletoe in winter.

# HELLO OWL

### YOU WILL NEED:

Embroidery hoop
18cm (7in)
Fusible web
Scraps of patterned fabric
Plain fabric
Embroidery thread
Fine jewellery or fuse wire

1. Trace each piece of the awl template separately onto fusible web. Iron onto the back of your patterned fabric scraps and cut out the pieces. Peel away the backing paper and assemble the owl on plain background fabric. Iron to fix into place.

2. Sew short, straight stitches randomly over the body and wing pieces to further secure the fabric and give a feathery texture. Add French knots for eyes and sew the legs into place below the body.

3. Twist some thin wire into shape and make a pair of glasses. Fix them in place over the owl's head with a few stitches at either side.

# FELT-TASTIC MR FOX

### YOU WILL NEED:

Embroidery hoop 18cm (7in)
Plain and patterned fabrics
Embroidery thread
Fusible web
Felt (black, white and tan)
Cocktail stick
Thin white card
Paper heart (optional)

1. Cut a 23cm (9in) square of patterned fabric and a 23cm x 7cm (9in x 2³⁄₄in) strip of brown fabric. Stitch the brown strip to the bottom of the larger piece. Copy the fox template pieces onto fusible web, iron onto felt and cut out. Assemble on the background, iron and then stitch in place. Use straight stitches on the head and body for 'fur'.

2. Cut a cocktail stick to 5cm (2in) long. Cut a 5cm x 1cm (2in x ³⁄₈in) strip of card with a notch in one end. Glue the opposite end to the top of the stick and add to the fox's hand. Decorate with a paper heart or message.

# TIME PIECE

## YOU WILL NEED:

Embroidery hoop 20cm (8in)
Four coordinating patterned fabrics
Heavyweight fusible interfacing
Thick card (e.g., recycled
from a cardboard box)
Clock movement (see Suppliers)
Wooden numbers

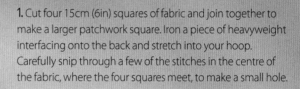

**1.** Cut four 15cm (6in) squares of fabric and join together to make a larger patchwork square. Iron a piece of heavyweight interfacing onto the back and stretch into your hoop. Carefully snip through a few of the stitches in the centre of the fabric, where the four squares meet, to make a small hole.

**2.** Cut thick card to fit into the recess at the back of the hoop. Make a hole in the middle for the spindle of your clock movement to fit through. Stick to the back of the fabric using double-sided tape.

**3.** Place the clock movement at the back of the hoop and carefully push the spindle through to the front. Screw the washers and hands into place, following the instructions on the packaging.

**4.** Glue wooden numbers together in layers of two or three for a chunky, dimensional effect. Fix to the clock face, positioning them over the seams in your fabric to mark the four quarters of an hour.

## TOP TIP

For extra security, fix the back part of the clock movement to the cardboard with a couple of adhesive foam pads.

# CHICKEN SCRATCH

## YOU WILL NEED:
Embroidery hoop 18cm (7in)
Gingham fabric
Embroidery thread (white, plus
a colour of your choice)

**1.** Working from the centre out, stitch the cross stitches, double cross stitches and French knots from the chart in the Template section onto gingham fabric.

Bring the white thread up at one corner of the central double cross stitch. Thread it under the cross stitch diagonally opposite and then back under the corner of the central stitch. The thread should form a long '0' shape. Repeat twice more.

**2.** To work the square loop stitches, bring the needle out at one corner of a double cross stitch. Thread it under the adjacent cross stitch and then the one diagonally opposite, the one adjacent to that and finally back through the original double cross stitch. Repeat twice, as before.

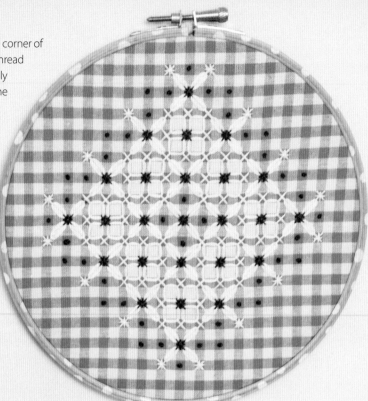

# LUCKY NUMBER

## YOU WILL NEED:
Embroidery hoop
15cm (6in)
Fusible web
Felt
Plain or patterned fabric

**1.** Print out numbers in your chosen font and at a large point size so they comfortably fill your hoop. Flip them as you print to get a reversed version of the image.

**2.** Trace over the numbers onto fusible web, iron onto felt and cut out. Iron to fix in place on your background fabric. To use as table numbers for a wedding or special event, display the finished hoop on a plate stand.

## TOP TIP
The font used for the figures in this hoop is Stöhr Numbers. Search online to download it for free, or try Modern No.20, which looks very similar.

**TOP TIP**

To re-size this project, make sure you measure the inside of the hoop to work out the necessary mirror size. If the mirror is too big, it won't fit into place. If, however, it's a bit on the small side, don't panic as you can always cover the gap with a strip of fancy braid or trim.

# MIRROR, MIRROR

**YOU WILL NEED:**

Embroidery hoop
13cm (5in)
Fabric
Round mirror 12cm (4³/₄in)
PVA glue
Double-sided adhesive
foam pads

**1.** Stretch a piece of fabric into your hoop. Turn the hoop to the back and trim the fabric, so you have just 2cm–3cm (³/₄in–1¹/₄in) excess all round.

**2.** Spread glue around the inside edges of the wood and neatly press the excess fabric down over it.

**3.** Fix double-sided adhesive foam pads to the back of your mirror. Peel away the backing strips and carefully press the mirror down into place in the centre of the frame.

# SOLAR SYSTEM

1. Cut strips of patterned fabric in the right shade for each planet (see chart). These can be as wide or as narrow as you like, depending on how many fabrics you're using and the size of the hoop.

2. Cut a piece of coordinating fabric that's 3cm–4cm (1¼in–1½in) bigger all round than your hoop. Take one of the fabric strips and sew it to the larger piece near the bottom edge. Take another strip and place on top so it just overlaps the stitching. Pin and then stitch to secure.

3. Keep going, layering up the strips until you've completely covered the backing fabric. Iron the work to remove any creases and then stretch into a decorated hoop.

4. To add rings to Saturn, sew a line of running stitches, roughly 1cm (³/₈in) long, diagonally across the centre of the hoop. Take the thread over and around the edges of the hoop at both ends of the stitched line.

5. If you are new to crochet refer to Techniques: Crochet. UK terms are used here. Use a 3mm–4mm (US D3–G6) crochet hook. Work two dc through each stitch, and four dc through the thread around each edge. To form the scalloped trim, chain one and then * skip one foundation stitch. Work five tr into the next stitch. Skip one foundation stitch and then work a dc into the next stitch. * Repeat from * to * all the way around.

| Planet | Hoop Size | Colour(s) |
|---|---|---|
| Mercury | 7.5cm (3in) | Grey |
| Venus | 13cm (5in) | Warm rich yellow |
| Earth | 15cm (6in) | Mid-blue and green |
| Mars | 10cm (4in) | Red and orange-red |
| Jupiter | 30cm (12in) | Orange, red and cream |
| Saturn | 25cm (10in) | Light yellow |
| Uranus | 20cm (8in) | Light aqua |
| Neptune | 20cm (8in) | Mid and pale blue |

*Planet sizes are only approximately to actual scale, so don't worry if you need to adjust them slightly.*

**TOP TIP**

Use a mixture of different hoop treatments to add interest, matching them to the fabric colours for each planet.

# BRANCHING OUT

**1.** Cut two rectangles of fabric, one 23cm x 18cm (9in x 7in) and one 23cm x 10cm (9in x 4in). With right sides facing, sew them together at one long edge. Press the seam flat. Stretch into a hoop (narrower strip at bottom) and copy the tree template on top. Stitch the outline and bark details into place.

**2.** Cut out twenty to twenty-five felt leaves in different green shades. Stitch to the fabric around the tree branches, using backstitch along the centre. Add clusters of French knots as blossom between the leaves and branches.

# STITCH THE DETAILS

**1.** Stretch fabric into your hoop and pick out the details you want to highlight or embellish.

**2.** Try stitching to emphasize outlines and edges, echoing shapes and details with coordinating thread or adding texture with filling stitches. Use as many or as few different stitches as you like to complement the design of the fabric.

## TOP TIP

Adjust the number of embroidery thread strands used to create different effects. One or two will give fine, subtle lines, while four or more will add more bulk and texture.

84

# RED BALLOON

## YOU WILL NEED:

Embroidery hoops 20cm
(8in) and 10cm (4in)
Plain and patterned fabrics
Embroidery thread
Fusible web
Pink marker pen
Red felt

## TOP TIP

Sew a pupil for each eye using black satin stitches. Add a tiny white straight stitch on top of each one so they look brighter and more alive.

1. Cut a 25cm (10in) square of blue fabric (plain or patterned) and stitch a smaller, curved piece at the bottom edge. Copy the template pieces onto fusible web, iron onto fabric or felt, as marked and then cut out. Set the balloon aside and assemble the remaining pieces on the fabric background before ironing into place.

2. Stitch around the edges of the dress and boots. Sew straight stitches across the socks to make stripes and then stitch facial features into place. Add dots of pink ink to each cheek.

3. Cut a 15cm (6in) square of the same blue fabric as before. Iron and stitch the balloon into place. Cut a white embroidery thread and knot one end. Bring the thread up at the base of the balloon and make a single stitch before bringing it back up at the same spot. Take the thread back down beside the girl's hand on the larger hoop so it looks as if she's flying the balloon. Secure the thread end at the back of the fabric.

# FABRIC CAMEO

## YOU WILL NEED:

Embroidery hoop 18cm (7in)
Patterned fabric
White or cream jersey fabric
Polyester stuffing or
wadding (batting)

### TOP TIP

Use a crochet hook to help you push stuffing into the nooks and crannies of the head.

**1.** Transfer the head template onto jersey fabric. Pin to a second layer of jersey and hand sew the pieces together, leaving a small gap. Trim away excess fabric and snip in towards the seams to ease around the curved parts of the design. Turn through the gap and stitch closed.

**2.** Sew the jersey head to the background fabric, slip stitching into place around the edges. Cut a slit in the background fabric, behind the head. Feed stuffing through the gap to pad out the head and sew shut.

# SHEER LAYERS

## YOU WILL NEED:

Embroidery hoop 18cm (7in)
Fusible web
Wide organza ribbon in mixture of colours
Dark grey embroidery thread

### TOP TIP

Try using marker pens to colour plain white organza ribbon. The alcohol-based ink will soak through the fibres like dye and be dry in a few minutes.

**1.** Draw eight to ten circles in a variety of sizes onto fusible web. Cut roughly around each one and iron onto a piece of organza ribbon. Cut out the circles more precisely and peel off the paper backing. Arrange on a plain white background, overlapping the circles in groups of two or three and then iron into place.

**2.** Sew irregular asterisk shapes around the circles using a single strand of dark grey thread.

# LACY-LIKE

## YOU WILL NEED:

Embroidery hoops 13cm (5in), 15cm (6in), 18cm (7in) and 20cm (8in)
Selection of lace trims
Invisible beading thread
A small metal ring (e.g., jewellery clasp or re-purposed finger ring)
Metal crimp beads and pliers

**1.** Discard the outer sections of the hoops. Spread glue around each hoop and press a strip of lace on top, overlapping the ends. Set aside to dry.

**2.** Cut four 150cm (60in) lengths of invisible thread. Fold in half and slide onto your hanging ring, securing each with a crimp bead just below the ring. Eight equal thread lengths should hang from the ring.

**3.** Take two of the threads and feed one through the lace in the largest hoop, from the outside in. Keep the other piece inside the hoop. Slide a crimp over both threads to join them together. Use pliers to close the crimp just inside the edge of the hoop, 20cm–25cm (8in–10in) below the hanging ring.

**4.** Repeat step three with the remaining threads, spacing them equally around the hoop. It should hang evenly from the ring at the top, kept in place by the crimps in each pair of threads.

**5.** Attach each pair of threads to the 18cm (7in) hoop in the same way. Allow a gap of 10cm–15cm (4in–6in) between the two hoops. Fix the final two hoops into place the same way. Trim excess thread to finish.

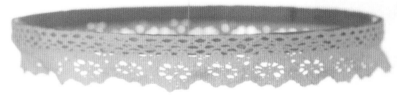

## TOP TIP

Crimps are small metal beads that can be squeezed together with pliers to make a firm closure. You could knot the threads instead, but it's easier to position crimps in precisely the right spot, keeping the hoops evenly suspended.

# MINI PHOTO ALBUM

## YOU WILL NEED:

Two embroidery hoops
each 10cm (4in)
Patterned fabric
Thin cardboard (e.g., recycled
from a cereal box)
Ribbon
Felt
Patterned paper
Chipboard letters and/or numbers
Ten to twelve photos

1. Draw around the inside of your hoop onto cardboard and cut out. Stretch patterned fabric into the hoop and slip the cardboard into the recess at the back. Fold over excess fabric at the back of the hoop and glue to the cardboard circle. Repeat with the second hoop.

2. Place the two hoops together, lining up the screws on the left-hand side, and with the neat side of the fabric facing outwards. Cut a 40cm (16in) length of ribbon. Fold in half to find the centre and place this between the hoop screws. Slip the rest of the ribbon between the hoops, pulling the ends out at the opposite side.

3. Carefully open out the hoops, leaving the ribbon in between the screws. Spread glue over the back of each one and press the middle part of each ribbon down on top. Cut two circles of felt and stick one to the back of each hoop, sandwiching the ribbons in place. When the glue dries, the ribbon between the screws should act like a hinge, joining them

together. The ribbon ends at the opposite side can be used to tie your album shut.

4. Decorate the side edges of each hoop with a strip of patterned paper. Add a date or name, reflecting the contents of your book to the front 'cover' hoop.

5. Cut your photos into 9cm (3½in) circles. Snip a 1m (1yd) length of sheer ribbon. Stick half of your photos along the ribbon, working from the centre out and leaving small gaps between. Turn over and stick another photo to the back of each one, so the ribbon is sandwiched between each back-to-back pair of pictures. Trim the remaining ribbon ends to 10cm (4in). Glue one to the back of each hoop, placing them horizontally across the centre.

6. Cut two 9cm (3½in) circles from patterned paper and glue one to the back of each hoop, covering the ribbon ends. When the glue is dry, the photos should work like pages, folding up accordion-style to fit neatly inside your book.

## TOP TIP

A mini-book like this is perfect for carrying in your handbag or pocket. Fill it with photos of your family or a special event, so you're ready to show them off at a moment's notice.

# MODULAR MARVEL

**YOU WILL NEED:**
Embroidery hoop 20cm (8in)
Thin card
Felt
Large button

**1.** Copy the flower petal onto thin card and use this as a template to cut out six felt petals. Take the first two and place them together with right sides facing. Sew along the dotted line from A to B.

**2.** Turn both felt pieces over, so the wrong sides are now facing, with the curved petal sections sandwiched between. Sew along the dotted line from B to C.

**3.** Join a third petal piece to the second one in the same way. Keep going until all six pieces are stitched together, forming a circle. Join the first and last pieces together, as before, to close the circle and finish your flower.

**4.** Press to iron all the petals open and the seams flat. Stretch into a decorated hoop, and glue or stitch a button over the centre of the flower.

**TOP TIP**
Don't worry if your petal pieces don't line up or meet exactly in the centre. The button will neatly (and sneakily) hide any imperfections from view.

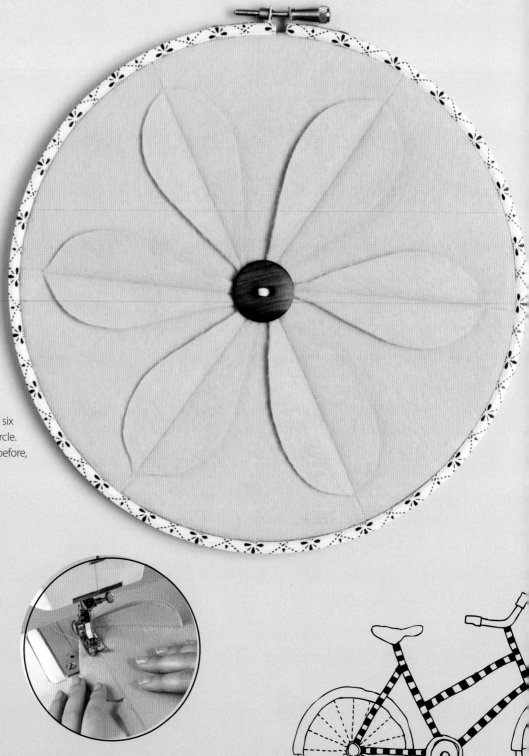

90

# BICYCLE WHEELS

## YOU WILL NEED:

Embroidery hoops: 20cm
(8in) and 13cm (5in)
Cream wool or yarn
Washi tape
Narrow double-sided adhesive tape
Silver thread
Thin card (plain or patterned)
Two shank buttons
Cocktail stick

**TOP TIP**
Use a self-cover button and scrap of fabric to add extra pattern to your wheel.

1. Separate the inner and outer sections of the large hoop. Crochet a chain stitch around the outer hoop using cream yarn (or wrap around instead) – see Techniques: Crochet. Cover the inner hoop with washi tape. Add double-sided tape over the washi, all the way around the outer edge.

2. Cut 25cm (10in) of silver thread, press one end down onto the tape and wrap it once around the hoop's edge. Stretch the thread tautly across to the opposite edge and wrap it around that side. Press the end firmly onto the sticky tape. Snip off excess.

3. Repeat, positioning a second thread at right angles to the first. Add more thread 'spokes' in the same way – eight thread lengths make sixteen spokes on each wheel, but you could add more.

4. Cut two 5cm (2in) circles of thin card and punch a hole in the centres. Spread glue over the back of both circles and press into place over the centre of the silver threads, one on the front and one on the back.

5. Push the button shank through the card centre holes, from front to back. Cut a short length of cocktail stick and push through the shank hole to hold the button in place on the front piece of card.

6. Join the two parts of the hoop back together again and tighten the screw. Make the second wheel using the smaller hoop in the same way.

# INITIAL THOUGHTS

**YOU WILL NEED:**

Embroidery hoops 10cm (4in),
13cm (5in) and/or 15cm (6in)
Plain and patterned fabric
Fusible web
Embroidery thread
Fancy braid or trim (optional)

**1.** To make block letters, print out your chosen initial in a bold, chunky font. Flip it as you print to get a reversed version. Trace over the letter onto fusible web, iron onto fabric and cut out. Iron to fix to your background. Hand or machine stitch around the edges.

**2.** For embroidered letters, pick a more delicate font, or draw the initial by hand. Trace onto fabric and stitch over the top using backstitch. Alternatively, trace a plainer initial onto fabric and sew a length of braid or trim into place over the outline.

**TOP TIP**

To reverse letters as you print, try selecting 'T-shirt transfers' (or similar) under Media Types in your printer options.

92

# CONVERSATIONAL

## YOU WILL NEED:

Embroidery hoop 18cm
(7in) and 13cm (5in)
Plain and patterned fabrics
Fusible web
Black embroidery thread
Felt
Letter stickers (optional)
Marker pen (optional)

1. Copy the template pieces onto fusible web, iron onto fabric and cut out. Set the T-shirt and speech bubble pieces aside. Iron the girl onto patterned background fabric. Use lines of machine stitching to fill in her hair, following the outline without worrying about being too neat.

2. Machine stitch the eyes, eyebrows and mouth into place and then use a single strand of thread to add eyelashes and nose. Fill in pupils with satin stitch, using black embroidery thread. Cut two circles of pink fabric and glue or stitch into place as cheeks.

3. Iron the T-shirt piece(s) into place and then stitch around the edges to secure. Cut out a felt bow, using the template as a guide, and glue into place over the hair.

4. Iron the speech bubble on to a separate piece of background fabric and sew around the edges to secure. Add your chosen text with letter stickers, embroidery or a marker pen.

## TOP TIP

It's easiesr to cut the T-shirt as a single piece but if you decide to use striped fabric, try cutting the arms out separately, so the stripes run in the right direction.

# OH, DEER

## YOU WILL NEED:

Embroidery hoop 20cm (8in)
Plain and/or patterned fabric
Black felt
Polyester stuffing or wadding (batting)
Pipe-cleaner
Medium or heavyweight interfacing

**1.** Copy the ear, antler and head templates onto patterned fabric and cut out. Place two of the ears together with right sides facing and stitch together around the side edges, leaving the bottom open. Turn the right way out and press. Repeat with the other two ear pieces.

**2.** With right sides facing, sew the two gusset pieces together along their shortest edges. Press the seam flat.

**3.** Pin an ear to the right side of each side-head piece, lining up raw edges. With right sides facing, pin the gusset to one of the side-head pieces, starting at point A and finishing at B (the ear should be sandwiched between the two layers of fabric). Hand sew the two pieces together.

**4.** Attach the remaining side-head piece to the opposite edge of the gusset in the same way. Cut in towards the seams to ease around the curved parts of the design and then turn the whole head the right way out and press.

**5.** Fill the head with stuffing, pushing it right down in to the nose end to create a good, well-padded shape. Don't worry that it's not sealed in at the back – you'll do this later, and will be able to add more stuffing or remove any excess later on. Cut a 2cm

**TOP TIP**

For a festive version of this project, turn the stag into a reindeer. Replace the black felt nose with a Rudolph-inspired red one, and for added cheer, decorate the antlers with jingle bells or mini baubles.

x 3cm (³⁄₄in x 1¹⁄₄in) piece of black felt and stitch into place over the end of the nose.

**6.** Cut two small circles of black felt for eyes. Glue one to each side of the head and then, using white thread, secure further with one or two tiny stitches in the centre. Take the thread through the full width of the head and pull gently as you sew from side to side, creating a small indent around each eye. This helps to give the head a more defined shape.

**7.** Pin and stitch the two antler pieces together, right sides facing, leaving a gap at the bottom. Clip curves, turn through the gap and press. Cut a 25cm (10in) piece of pipe-cleaner and push inside the antlers. Fill the remaining space with stuffing, pushing it in to all the gaps with a crochet hook or blunt pencil. Sew the gap shut and stitch the antlers to the top of the head.

**8.** Iron interfacing onto the reverse of your background fabric and stretch into a hoop. Fold over a 2cm (³⁄₄in) hem along all open edges at the back of the stag head. Pin to the fabric in the hoop, keeping the head positioned as centrally as possible. Adjust the amount of stuffing if necessary at this point. Slip stitch around all edges to hold in place before removing the pins.

# CONCENTRIC SAMPLER

## YOU WILL NEED:

Embroidery hoop
18cm (7in)
Compass
Erasable fabric pen
Fusible interfacing
Embroidery threads

### TOP TIP
This project is a great chance to try out new embroidery stitches, or those you know but don't get to use very often.

1. Use a compass and an erasable fabric pen to mark a series of concentric circles on your fabric. Iron interfacing onto the back to stabilize the fabric. Stretch into a hoop.

2. Work your chosen stitches over, or between, the various circles. Try couching, French knots, running, chain, straight, cross, back or feather stitches (see Techniques: Embroidery Stitches). Mix them up to create more unusual effects. Finish off with a French knot and lazy daisy stitches in the centre.

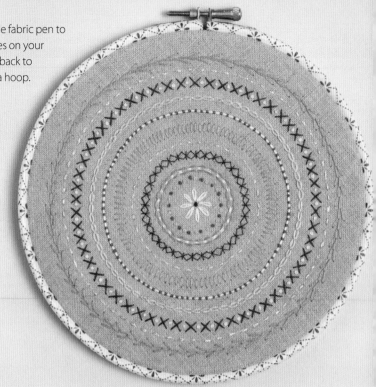

# FRENCH SHADING

## YOU WILL NEED:

Embroidery hoop 15cm (6in)
Patterned fabric
Erasable fabric marker pen
Embroidery threads

### TOP TIP
Try the same technique with other simple shapes, such as hearts, stars or initials.

1. Copy the template onto patterned fabric with an erasable marker. Stitch over the outline using French knots, matching the thread colour to the fabric colour. For instance, if the outline goes over a white part of the fabric, cover that part of the line with white knots. If it then crosses over into a red part of the fabric, change to red knots.

2. Once you've outlined the shape, carry on stitching. Fill in the whole shape with French knots, matching the colours to shadow the pattern on the fabric as you go.

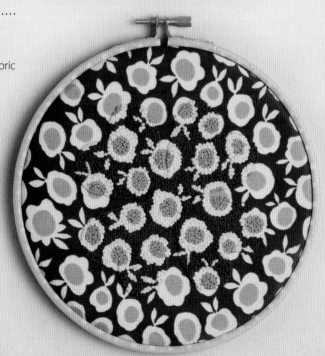

# DEAR DIORAMA

**YOU WILL NEED:**
Embroidery hoop 18cm (7in)
Card or mount board
Patterned paper/thin card (e.g.,
scrapbooking papers)
White felt
Adhesive foam pads
Fine black marker pen

**1.** Discard the inner part of your hoop and tighten the screw to close the gap at the top of the outer section. Place it on a piece of card and draw around the outside edge. Cut out the card circle.

**2.** Cover the circle with blue paper and glue it to the back of the hoop. Cut a semicircle of white felt and stick into position at the bottom of the hoop.

**3.** Cut a selection of triangles from thin card to make mountains. Glue a few flat against the background and then add the others using adhesive foam pads. Cut cloud shapes from light-coloured paper and stick to the sky.

**4.** Draw fir trees onto thin green card (use the template as a guide, but try to copy them freehand so they don't look too uniform). Cut out and then cut and fold extra strips of card, as shown on the template. Glue one to the back of each tree before adding to the background in front of the mountains.

**5.** Copy the bear template onto white card and cut out. Add a scarf and a folded strip of card behind to help him perch at the front edge of the hoop.

# MATRYOSHKA

## YOU WILL NEED:

Embroidery hoops 13cm (5in), 15cm
(6in), 18cm (7in) and 20cm (8in)
Fusible web
Plain and patterned fabrics
Felt
Scraps of ribbon and lace
Embroidery thread
Erasable fabric marker

**1.** Copy the templates onto fusible web, iron onto felt or fabric, as marked, and cut out. Set the felt hoods aside. Assemble the remaining pieces of each doll on patterned background fabric and then iron into place.

**2.** Sew around the outside of the doll bodies and any decorative or trimming pieces. Copy a face onto each one using an erasable marker and then backstitch over the top. Sew French knots in pink thread to make rosy cheeks.

**3.** Iron the hood into place on each doll. Sew around the outer edge in coordinating thread and then add running stitches around the inner opening in a contrasting colour.

## TOP TIP

If you don't want to hang these as a set of four hoops, reduce the template sizes and stitch all four dolls across the centre of a single large hoop instead.

98

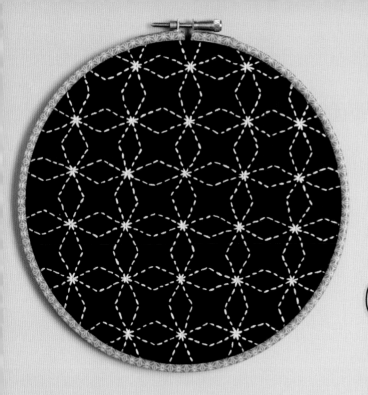

# SIMPLE SASHIKO

## YOU WILL NEED:

Embroidery hoop 18cm (7in)
Navy blue fabric
Dressmaker's carbon paper
Ball-point pen
White embroidery thread

### TOP TIP

Sashiko is a traditional form of Japanese embroidery, usually stitched in white on an indigo background, but you could easily change the colours to suit your style or décor.

1. Iron the blue fabric and place on a firm surface, with dressmaker's carbon on top. Copy the sashiko template onto plain paper. Place this on top of the carbon and trace firmly over the lines with a ball-point pen to transfer the design.

2. Stitch over the lines using two or three strands of white embroidery thread and a running stitch. Where the stitches meet at the ends of each diamond motif, they will form an asterisk shape.

# COFFEE TIME

## YOU WILL NEED:

Embroidery hoop 20cm (8in)
Plain and patterned fabrics
Fusible web
Erasable fabric marker
Sewing thread (black and white)

### TOP TIP

You can do this kind of machine embroidery with a standard presser foot but for a clearer view as you're stitching, try using a zipper foot instead.

1. Cut two rectangles of fabric, one 17cm x 25cm (6¾in x 10in) and one 11cm x 25cm (4¼in x 10in). With right sides facing, sew together at one long edge. Press the seam flat. Draw two 5cm (2in) circles onto fusible web. Iron onto patterned fabric and cut out. Peel off the backing and iron one onto each side of the background fabric.

2. With the seam between the two fabrics at an angle, trace the coffee pot from the template onto your fabric. Machine stitch over the outline in black thread. Stitch around the outer edges of both circles, by hand or machine, with white thread.

# PAPER SHISHA

**YOU WILL NEED:**
Embroidery hoop 18cm (7in)
Cardboard
Patterned paper
Plain or patterned fabric
Embroidery thread

**1.** Cut out ten card circles 2cm–3cm (¾in–1¼in) in diameter. Cover each one with patterned paper to decorate.

**2.** Place one of the circles on the background fabric and stitch a grid of four stitches over the top to hold in place (these stitches are shown in green on picture detail 1). Now sew a second grid of stitches over the top at right angles to the first (stitches shown in blue).

**3.** Bring your needle up at the circle edge, at point A on picture 2 (stitches shown in red). Pass it over then under the holding stitches, as shown, keeping the thread to the left of the needle. Take the needle back down through point A and out through point B, still with the thread on the left. Pull taut to finish off the stitch.

**4.** Pass the needle over then under the holding stitches again, down through point B and up at point C (picture 3), keeping the thread under the needle to the left.

**5.** Working in the same way, stitch all around the edge of the circle. Back at the starting place, take the needle back down through point A and secure the thread at the back of the fabric. Sew the rest of the circles to the background fabric in the same way.

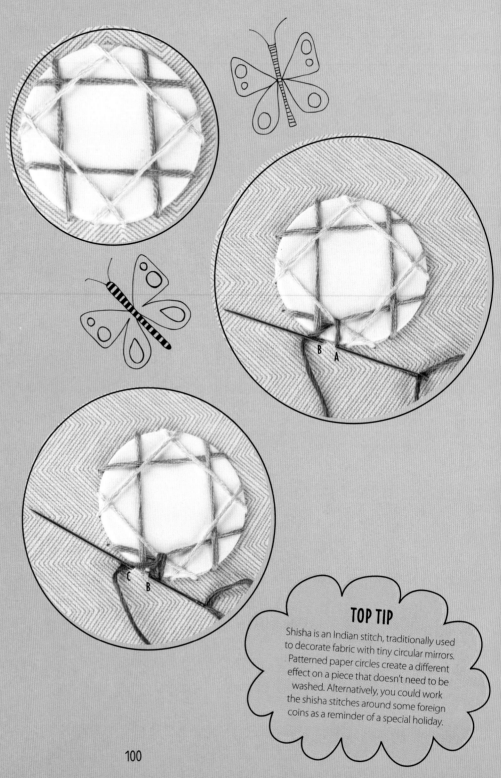

## TOP TIP

Shisha is an Indian stitch, traditionally used to decorate fabric with tiny circular mirrors. Patterned paper circles create a different effect on a piece that doesn't need to be washed. Alternatively, you could work the shisha stitches around some foreign coins as a reminder of a special holiday.

# BORDER LINES

### YOU WILL NEED:

Embroidery hoop 18cm (7in)
Fusible web
Plain and patterned fabrics
Embroidery thread
Yarn
Acrylic paint

**1.** Trace the bird template onto fusible web, iron onto patterned fabric and cut out. Iron into place on the background fabric. Stitch on a sleepy eye and backstitch around the edges. Add two lengths of yarn for legs, holding in place with couching stitches.

**2.** Paint a hoop the same colour as the background fabric and leave to dry. Stretch the fabric into place. Sew a line of evenly spaced French knots around the outer edge. Add two open chain stitches between each knot, to look like tiny leaves.

### TOP TIP

By matching the hoop and fabric colours, the stitched border becomes the frame for your design. Try it with other patterns too.

# FEATHER-LIKE

### YOU WILL NEED:

Embroidery hoop 20cm (8in)
Plain or patterned fabric
Erasable fabric marker
Embroidery thread
Feather (real or craft)

**1.** Transfer the feather templates onto your fabric using an erasable marker. Leave a gap to add the real feather later on. Use two or three close-set lines of split stitch to make a stalk for each feather and then work the remainder in satin stitch.

**2.** Apply a thin line of glue to the centre back of your real feather and press it down into place on the fabric.

### TOP TIP

Set the satin stitches slightly further apart than you normally would for the ombre and banded feathers to give them a more realistic feathery effect.

# REVERSE APPLIQUÉ

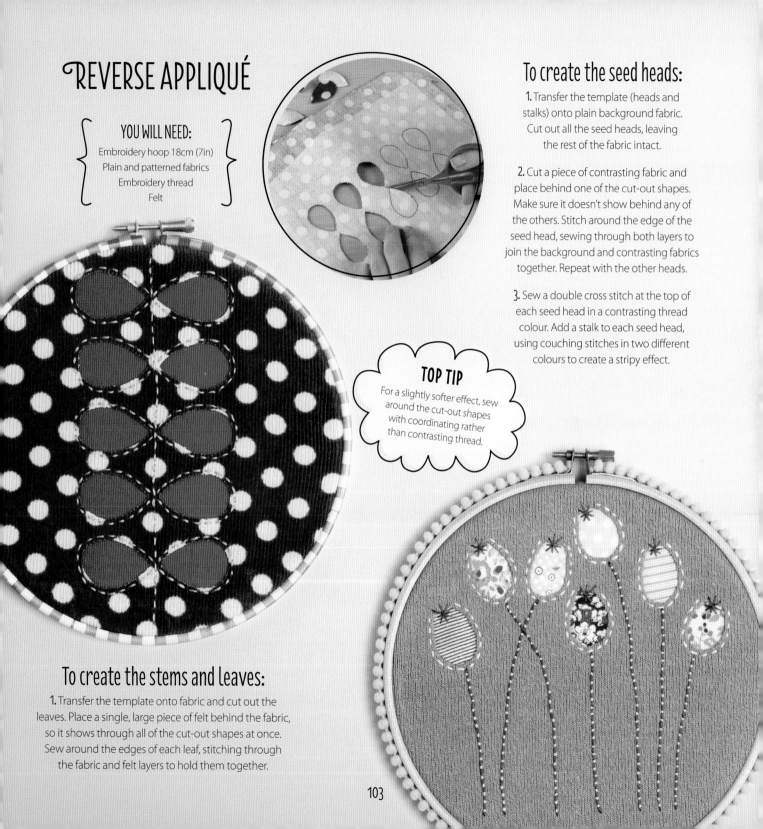

## YOU WILL NEED:

Embroidery hoop 18cm (7in)
Plain and patterned fabrics
Embroidery thread
Felt

## To create the seed heads:

1. Transfer the template (heads and stalks) onto plain background fabric. Cut out all the seed heads, leaving the rest of the fabric intact.

2. Cut a piece of contrasting fabric and place behind one of the cut-out shapes. Make sure it doesn't show behind any of the others. Stitch around the edge of the seed head, sewing through both layers to join the background and contrasting fabrics together. Repeat with the other heads.

3. Sew a double cross stitch at the top of each seed head in a contrasting thread colour. Add a stalk to each seed head, using couching stitches in two different colours to create a stripy effect.

## TOP TIP

For a slightly softer effect, sew around the cut-out shapes with coordinating rather than contrasting thread.

## To create the stems and leaves:

1. Transfer the template onto fabric and cut out the leaves. Place a single, large piece of felt behind the fabric, so it shows through all of the cut-out shapes at once. Sew around the edges of each leaf, stitching through the fabric and felt layers to hold them together.

# RUB-ON TRANSFERS

## YOU WILL NEED:
Embroidery hoop 18cm (7in)
Acrylic paint
Rub-on transfers
Lollipop stick (often supplied with the transfers)
Plain fabric
Embroidery threads

**1.** Brush one or two coats of acrylic paint on the hoop and allow to dry. Cut out transfers one at a time and remove the protective covering. Position on the hoop and rub on firmly with a lollipop stick. Remove the backing paper. Add more transfers to build up your design around the whole hoop or in smaller sections.

**2.** Trace the banner template onto fabric and stitch around the outline. Satin stitch the heart. Write or print and trace two sets of initials, one either side of the heart. Sew with a contrasting thread colour in whipped backstitch.

# BEADED BUTTERFLY

## YOU WILL NEED:
Embroidery hoop 15cm (6in)
Medium to heavyweight fabric
Seed beads and bugle beads
Six larger beads
Beading needle
Fine wire

**1.** Transfer the butterfly template onto your fabric. Stitch a row of horizontal bugle beads into place to make the body. Sew three larger beads to each wing, keeping the design symmetrical.

**2.** Stitch a mixture of bugle and seed beads over the outlined wings. Add a second line inside the first and keep going, moving towards the centre until the whole shape is filled. Snip a length of wire to make the antennae. Fold it in half and slip behind the body.

## TOP TIP
To sew the seed beads into place, work lines of backstitch, slipping a bead onto your needle before you make each stitch.

# CHRISTMAS WREATH

**YOU WILL NEED:**

Embroidery hoop 18cm (7in)
Double-sided adhesive tape
White yarn
Beads and sequins (white, crystal/
clear, silver and wooden)
Small jingle bells
Silver glitter ribbon

1. Tighten the hoop screw to hold the inner and outer sections together as firmly as possible. Cut a long strip of double-sided tape and wrap around the hoop (treating the inner and outer sections as one). Peel away the backing paper and wrap yarn around the hoop, keeping the strands as close together as you can. Press it down onto the sticky tape as you go. When you've covered the first strip of tape, add more and keep going until the whole hoop is wrapped.

2. Tie a length of white sewing thread to one side of the hoop and slide on a bead, sequin or bell. Add a dot of glue underneath before wrapping the thread around the hoop again. Check you're happy with the placement of the bead and then add another in the same way. Mix up shapes and sizes as you thread them on, adding glue under each one to hold it in place. Tie off the thread when it runs short and carry on with a new piece.

3. When you've covered the whole wreath, tie a length of silver ribbon into a bow and glue it over the screw at the top of the hoop.

# JOINED AT THE HIP

**1.** Position the hinge centrally against the side edge of one hoop. Hold firmly in place and push a screw into the hoop – the wood should be soft enough to make a small hole (see picture detail 1). Tighten the screw with a screwdriver, so it goes through the inner and outer part of the hoop. Repeat with another screw at the opposite end of the hinge.

**2.** Repeat step one to fix the other side of the hinge to your second hoop. Now remove all four screws and set the hinges aside so you have two separate hoops again.

**3.** Copy the templates onto fusible web and iron onto felt or fabric, as marked. Cut out and then assemble and iron on to your background fabric. Sew around the edges and stitch the facial features into place.

**4.** Stretch each piece of decorated fabric into one of the hoops. Re-screw the hinge into place, using the same holes you made at the start (picture 2). Finish the back of the hoops as you normally would and then cover the back of each one with a piece of felt so the ends of the screws are hidden from view.

**TOP TIP**

The hinges are added first because you need to push down very firmly to make the initial screw holes. Doing this with the fabric in position is likely to pull or twist it out of shape.

# TECHNIQUES

This section contains all you need to know about the embroidery, appliqué, patchwork and crochet techniques used on the projects.

## Embroidery

### GETTING STARTED

Thread your needle. To make a knot in the end of the thread, wrap it around your finger in a loop and feed the end through the loop a couple of times. Pull taut to make the knot, and then snip away any excess thread beneath it. Take your needle through the fabric, from back to front, pulling the thread until the knot sits neatly behind the fabric.

### EMBROIDERY THREADS

Embroidery thread – sometimes known as floss or stranded cotton – is made up of six separate strands. Although you can sew with all six, it's often more effective to separate them. To do this, hold the thread up and use your fingers to pull the strands apart at the top. Hold on to the strands you want to pull away in one hand, and hold the rest in the other. Gently start to pull the two groups apart, pressing one of your index fingers down into the V shape that forms between them to ease tangles or resistance.

- Use a single strand of thread for very fine details, such as facial features on small projects. One strand can also be used to create a more subtle outline on larger pieces.
- Two strands will create a fine line on projects of most sizes, and for small French knots.

- Using three strands is the most common way to split a length of embroidery thread. It's a good, general-purpose thickness and perfect for beginners getting to grips with embroidery.
- Four strands will create a thicker, bolder line on your projects and can be useful for adding interesting texture.
- Five or six strands will give you a chunky look on all but the largest of pieces. It's useful if you need stitches to show up clearly on thicker fabrics, such as wool or velvet, but can be tricky to sew through jersey and very fine cottons.

### FINISHING OFF

When you reach the end of the stitched design, or run out of thread, tie it off securely at the back, either with a knot, or by threading through the back of the last few stitches worked.

### EMBROIDERY STITCHES

Various embroidery stitches are used throughout the book. All are easy to work and are described and shown here.

#### Backstitch

- Make a single straight stitch and then bring your needle back up through the fabric a stitch length away.
- Take the thread back down through the end of the first stitch.
- Bring your needle up a stitch length away from the end of the second stitch.
- Take it back down through the end of the second stitch. Keep going to build up a smooth, solid line of stitches.

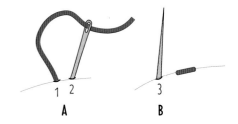

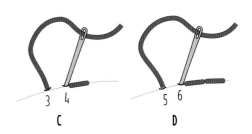

#### Chain Stitch

- Bring your thread up through the fabric (point A), and hold it down with your left thumb. Take the needle back down through point 1, leaving a loop. Bring the needle up a stitch length away at point 2.
- Keeping the thread under your needle, pull through to form your first chain stitch.
- Hold the thread down with your thumb, as before, and take the needle back through point 2. Bring it up a stitch length away and pull through. Keep going to build up a full chain.

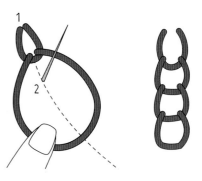

- **Couching**

- Place a thick piece of braid, thread or yarn on top of the fabric. Using two to three strands of embroidery thread bring your needle up at one side of the braid.

- Take it back down on the opposite side and pull through so the stitch is wrapped around the braid.

- Keep going, adding stitches at regular intervals to hold the thicker braid in place on the surface of the fabric.

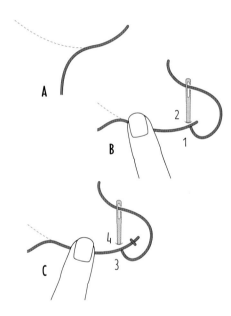

### Cross Stitch

- Working on a counted-thread fabric, such as Aida, bring your needle up through one of the holes (number 1 on diagram A). Count two threads across and two down and take the thread back down (2), making a diagonal stitch.

- Count two threads across and bring your needle back up (3). Now count two threads across and two up and take the thread back down (4) to finish the stitch.

- Make another stitch in the same way, starting at the top left corner of the previous stitch.

- To work cross stitches on gingham fabric, use the squares as a guide, rather than counting threads. On plain fabric, just stitch each X freehand, leaving small gaps in between for an irregular but pretty effect.

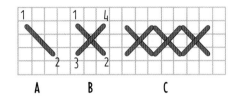

### Detached Chain Stitch/Lazy Daisy

- Work a single chain stitch and then take your thread back down through the fabric to form a tiny straight stitch over the end of the chain.

- You can either work these stitches singly or, more commonly, arrange them in a circular group of five or six to form the petals of a lazy daisy.

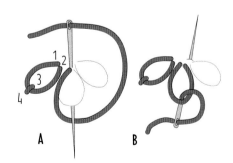

### Double Cross Stitch

- Work a single cross stitch and then count one thread across and bring the needle back up. Count two threads down and take the thread back through the fabric vertically.

- Bring it back out, one thread up and one thread across, and then count two threads across and take it back through the fabric horizontally to finish the stitch.

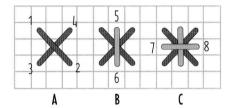

### Feather Stitch

- This stitch is made up of a series of loops, each anchored by the following stitch. The pattern of loops swings alternately to the right and left to create a staggered pattern.

- Lightly mark four removable vertical lines on your fabric, about 5mm (¼in) apart. If you want to be really accurate, mark a 5mm (¼in) grid (shown in blue on diagrams).

- Follow diagram A, bringing the thread up at 1 and down at 2, leaving a loop. Bring the needle up at 3 (over the loop, which will anchor it), down at 4 and up again at 5.

- Follow diagram B, taking the needle down at 6 and up at 7, over the loop of thread.

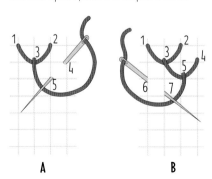

- Follow diagram C, going down at 8 and up at 9, again forming a loop. You'll see that each loop is anchored by the next stitch.
- Continue in this way, swinging the stitch to the left, then right and so on. When you want to finish the run of feather stitch, sew a final small stitch to anchor the last loop (D).

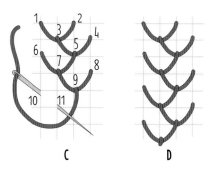

C          D

### French Knots

- Bring your needle up through the fabric and wrap the thread around the needle two or three times.
- Holding the thread taut, push the point of your needle back down through the fabric close to the start of the stitch.
- Still keeping the thread taut on the right side of the work, pull the needle through to the back, leaving a small knot on the surface of the fabric.

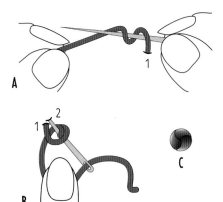

### Running Stitch

- Bring your needle up through the fabric and then take it back down a stitch length away (you can make stitches long or short, as preferred).
- Bring it back up at roughly the same distance apart and then make a second stitch in the same way. Continue to build up an even row of stitches with evenly sized gaps between.

### Satin Stitch

- This is usually worked to fill in an outline drawn onto your fabric. Start by bringing the needle up at one side of the outline. Take it back down at the opposite side, making a straight stitch.
- Make another straight stitch next to the first one, keeping them as close together as possible.
- Keep adding stitches, following the drawn outline until you've filled the whole shape.

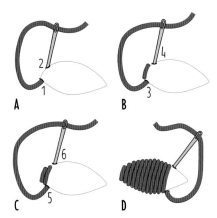

### Split Stitch

- This stitch works like a backstitch/ chain stitch hybrid and can generally be used as an alternative to either.
- Bring your needle up through the fabric and back down again to form a single stitch. Bring the needle back up through the centre of the stitch, so it splits the thread.
- Take your needle back down, forming a second stitch and then come back up through the centre again. Carry on, making and splitting stitches to form a smooth line.

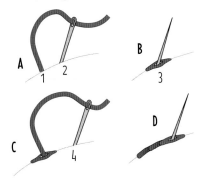

### Whipped Backstitch

- The 'whipped' part of this stitch can be the same colour as the backstitch or a different colour.
- Sew a line of backstitches and then bring your thread back out at the start of the line.
- Slide your needle under the first stitch, working from top to bottom, and pull the thread taut.
- Repeat, sliding the needle under the second stitch from top to bottom. Keep going 'whipping' the thread through each stitch.

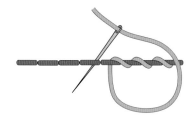

# Appliqué

The appliqué projects in this book use fusible web to fix smaller fabric shapes to a plain or patterned background. Fusible web is a heat-activated adhesive with a paper backing, generally used to fix two or more layers of fabric together. You can buy it in packaged sheets or by the metre/yard. The main difference between this method and more traditional appliqué is that fabric edges are left raw and unfinished. Fraying is minimal as the fusible web helps to seal edges. If you're bothered by rough edges, stick to materials such as felt and jersey, which don't fray, or tight-weave fabrics such as cotton lawn or broadcloth, which will fray less.

## TRANSFERRING DESIGNS

Designs can be traced onto the backing paper of the fusible web. Place the web over your chosen template and trace with a soft pencil. Note that the image will be reversed when you apply it to fabric. If it's not symmetrical, or if you want the design to face in a particular direction, you will need to flip the image before tracing. To do this, copy onto normal tracing paper using a black marker pen, turn the paper over and then re-trace onto the fusible web.

## APPLYING TO FABRIC

Once your design is in place, cut it out roughly, leaving a narrow border outside the pencil lines. Iron the fabric to remove creases and then iron fusible web onto the back, with the paper side facing up – the web underneath it is the part that will stick to the fabric. With the paper backing still in place, cut out the shape, following the pencil outline. Peel off the paper and position the piece on the background, web side face down. Iron over the top to fuse it to the background fabric.

## STITCHING IN PLACE

On decorative projects that aren't going to be washed or get daily use and wear, the fusible web will hold appliqué pieces in place. However, for added security and also to highlight or embellish the design you can stitch your appliqué into place, too. The stitching used will depend on the project.

### Outlining by hand

Sew around the outer edges using a running or backstitch. Toning thread gives a subtle effect, while a contrasting shade makes a bigger statement.

### Outlining by machine

Sew around the outer edges of your piece using a straight machine stitch, working as close to the raw edges of the fabric as you can. Adding a second row gives a bolder look and can help to mask any imperfections.

### Overstitching

Use tiny straight stitches worked over the edges of the appliquéd piece, from the outside in. This is especially effective on felt, where the stitches will almost melt into the edges of the material.

### Detail or all-over stitching

Work stitches in a pattern or randomly across the whole surface of the fabric, for instance to represent fur on animals. This method can be combined with any of those above, but even on its own is enough to hold a piece in place. As before, it can be worked in coordinating or contrasting threads, depending on the look you're trying to create.

## BUILDING LAYERS

Appliqué designs can be worked as a single layer or built up over a number of layers to create a more detailed image. To layer an appliqué design, transfer all of the template pieces onto fusible web, iron onto fabric and then cut out, as described before. Peel off the backing paper and assemble the pieces to check your design. When you're happy with how it looks, place the bottom layer on your background fabric and iron into position. Add the next layer on top, and iron again. Keep going, ironing one layer into place at a time, until the whole thing is in place and then add stitching to secure.

## TOP TIP

If you accidentally iron the tacky side of fusible web, turn your iron off at once. Allow it to cool and then wipe the surface plate clean. Test on scrap fabric when you turn it back on to make sure you've removed the stickiness.

# Crochet

## CROCHET ABBREVIATIONS

Crochet terms vary in different parts of the world and the same name can be used for two completely different stitches. This book uses UK terms throughout but see the conversion chart for USA terms.

| UK | USA |
| --- | --- |
| st (stitch) | st (stitch) |
| sl st (slip stitch) | sl st (slipped stitch) |
| ch (chain) | ch (chain) |
| dc (double crochet) | sc (single crochet) |
| tr (treble crochet) | dc (double crochet) |

## CASTING ON (MAKING A SLIP-LOOP)

- Instructions are for a right-handed person. If you are left-handed hold the hook in your left hand and manipulate the yarn in your right. hand

- Make a loop in the yarn and grip it between your thumb and forefinger. Hold the tail end out of the way in your left hand.

- Holding the crochet hook in your right hand, insert it through the loop. Catch the yarn underneath and pull it back up with the hook.

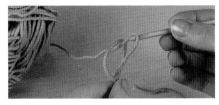

- Holding both the tail and the ball end of the yarn in your left hand, carry on pulling upwards to create a loop on your hook. Slide the knot up so it sits snugly just below the loop.

## CHAIN STITCH (ch)

- Make a slip-loop, as before. Wrap the yarn around your hook and, catching it in the lip of the hook, pull through the loop.

- Make as many more chain stitches as you need in the same way.

## SLIP STITCH (sl st)

- Insert your hook through the stitch specified in the pattern. Wrap the yarn around, and pull it back through the stitch and the loop on the hook.

## DOUBLE CROCHET (dc)

- Insert your crochet hook through the stitch or gap. Wrap yarn around the hook and pull it back through the stitch. You should now have two loops on the hook.

- Wrap the yarn around your hook again, and pull it back through both of the loops.

## TREBLE CROCHET (tr)

- Wrap the yarn around your hook.

- Insert the hook through the specified stitch. Wrap the yarn around the hook again and pull it back through the stitch. There should now be three loops on the hook.

- Wrap the yarn around your hook and pull it back through two of the loops.

- Wrap the yarn around one more time and pull it back through the last two loops.

## CASTING OFF

- Cut the yarn 15cm (6in) from the hook. Hook the yarn through the last loop worked and pull to secure. Trim the yarn end.

## Patchwork

### CHOOSING FABRIC

Most patchwork is done using lightweight cotton fabric but unless you're planning to regularly wash your finished hoop project, you have more leeway to mix different fabrics than if you were making something like a patchwork quilt. Select colours and patterns that coordinate, maybe sticking to prints from the same fabric range if you find it tricky to mix and match different designs. Go with a limited colour palette to create a muted, cohesive impression, or use a wider range of shades for a more eclectic look.

### PLANNING YOUR DESIGN

Patchwork pieces can be cut in all kinds of different shapes, including triangles, diamonds and hexagons. However, to begin with, it's probably best to stick with squares or rectangles. Squares are ideal for regular, grid-like designs, while rectangles allow for more variety and can be a little more forgiving of inaccuracies or imperfect stitching. Try sketching your design onto scrap paper before you start cutting fabric. Bear in mind that while it's fine to vary them in width, all pieces in the same row should ideally be the same height.

### CUTTING OUT

Many patchwork enthusiasts cut their fabric using a rotary cutter and mat. This creates beautifully accurate cuts, quickly and simply. However, for small-scale projects, scissors and a ruler are just as effective. Draw your patchwork pieces directly onto fabric with an erasable marker and then cut out.

### CREATING ARRANGEMENTS

Arrange the patchwork pieces on a flat surface to check that your design works. Once you're happy with the placement of the fabric pieces, take a quick photo or make a note of the order so you don't lose track as you begin to sew.

### STITCHING TOGETHER

- Take the first two patchwork pieces and pin together with right sides facing. Sew along the edge, keeping your seam quite narrow, about 1cm (³⁄₈in). Press the seam to one side.

- If you're using dark-coloured fabric next to a lighter shade, press the seam towards the darker side so it doesn't show through the light fabric.

- Add your next piece in the same way and then keep going until you've joined all the pieces in a single row.

- Join the pieces in the next row, using the same method. When you've finished, place the two rows of patchwork together with right sides facing. Sew along the edge, again keeping your seam quite narrow. Press the seam, as before.

- Continue building rows, and adding them to your patchwork until you have a single patchworked square large enough for a hoop.

# TEMPLATES & MOTIFS

All of the templates and motifs you will need for the projects are included in this section. Page references for the templates can be found on the Contents page. In general, the template sizes have been chosen to fit specific hoop sizes but you can adjust the sizes if you chose. **Important note:** the templates have been reduced by half to fit the book, so enlarge on a photocopier by 200%.

**MY ONLY SUNSHINE**
Clouds

**RETRO RABBIT**

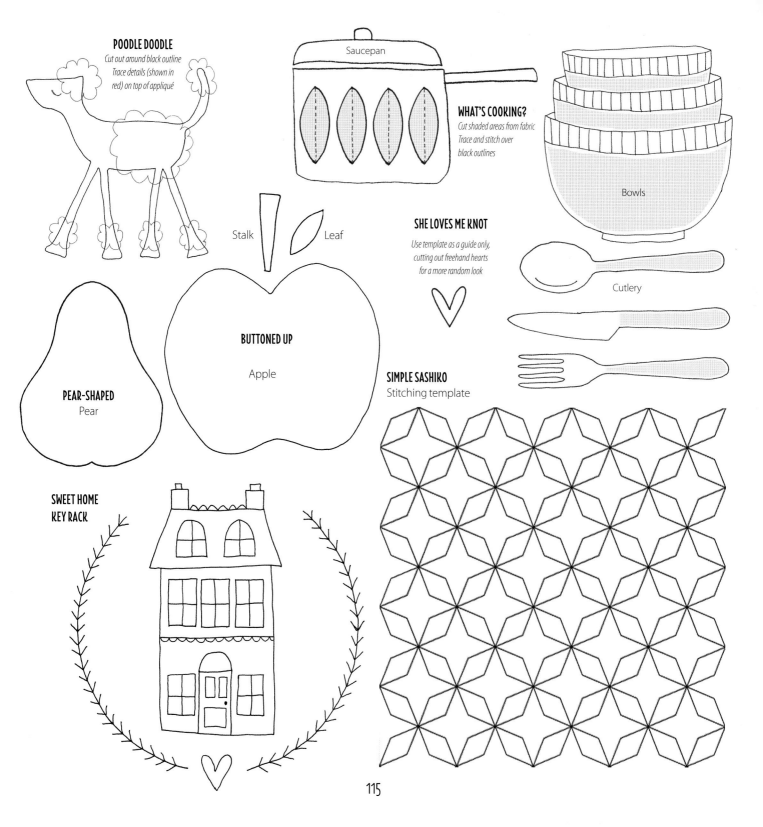

**POODLE DOODLE**
*Cut out around black outline*
*Trace details (shown in red) on top of appliqué*

Saucepan

**WHAT'S COOKING?**
*Cut shaded areas from fabric*
*Trace and stitch over black outlines*

Bowls

Stalk          Leaf

**SHE LOVES ME KNOT**
*Use template as a guide only, cutting out freehand hearts for a more random look*

Cutlery

**BUTTONED UP**

Apple

**PEAR-SHAPED**
Pear

**SIMPLE SASHIKO**
Stitching template

**SWEET HOME KEY RACK**

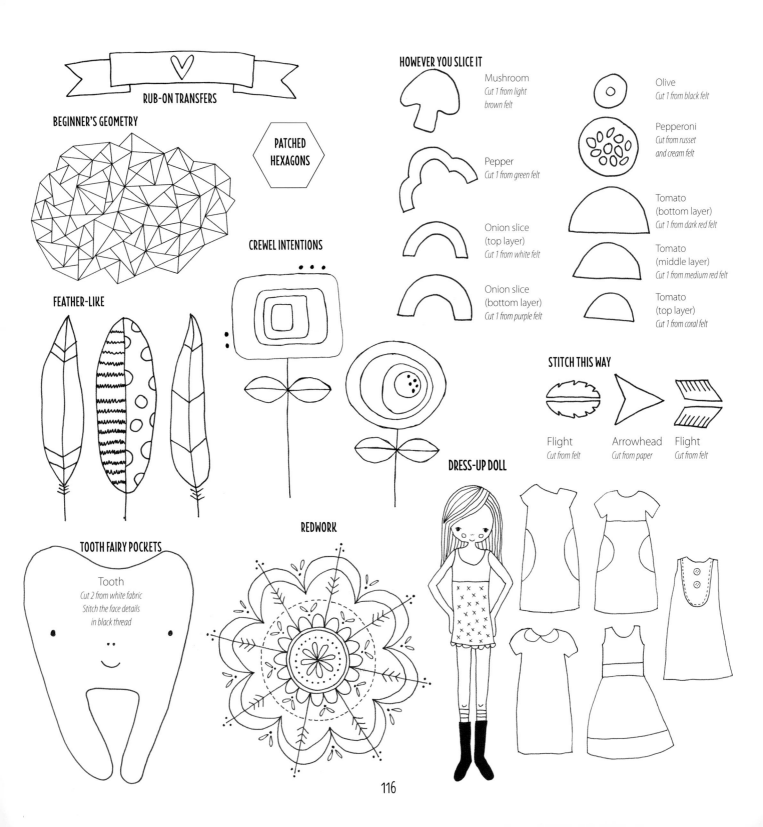

RUB-ON TRANSFERS

BEGINNER'S GEOMETRY

PATCHED HEXAGONS

CREWEL INTENTIONS

FEATHER-LIKE

TOOTH FAIRY POCKETS

Tooth
*Cut 2 from white fabric*
*Stitch the face details*
*in black thread*

REDWORK

HOWEVER YOU SLICE IT

Mushroom
*Cut 1 from light*
*brown felt*

Pepper
*Cut 1 from green felt*

Onion slice
(top layer)
*Cut 1 from white felt*

Onion slice
(bottom layer)
*Cut 1 from purple felt*

Olive
*Cut 1 from black felt*

Pepperoni
*Cut from russet*
*and cream felt*

Tomato
(bottom layer)
*Cut 1 from dark red felt*

Tomato
(middle layer)
*Cut 1 from medium red felt*

Tomato
(top layer)
*Cut 1 from coral felt*

STITCH THIS WAY

Flight
*Cut from felt*

Arrowhead
*Cut from paper*

Flight
*Cut from felt*

DRESS-UP DOLL

# STITCHED SILHOUETTE

&

## LACECAPS

### Stalks
*Cut from felt*

### Mushroom caps
*Cut whole shape from felt*
*Cut area above dotted line from patterned fabric*

## UP AND AWAY
Balloon centre

## MIX TAPE SCREENPRINTS

## TYPEWRITTEN

### Paper
*Cut 1 from fabric*
*Insert lower edge*
*through gap in backing*
*piece, up to dotted line*

### Backing
*Cut 1 from black or dark grey felt*
*Cut along red line and slip*
*'paper' through gap*

### Handle
*Trace and stitch*
*directly onto fabric*

### Front
*Cut both pieces from patterned fabric*
*Stitch along dotted lines to add detail*

### Space bar
*Cut 1 from felt*
*Stitch along dotted*
*lines to add detail*

### Wheel
*Cut 1 from felt*

## MULTI-HOOP ZOO

### Dog front body
*Cut 1 front body (without ear) from fabric*
*Cut 2 ear pieces from contrasting fabric*

### Dog back body
*Cut 1 from fabric*

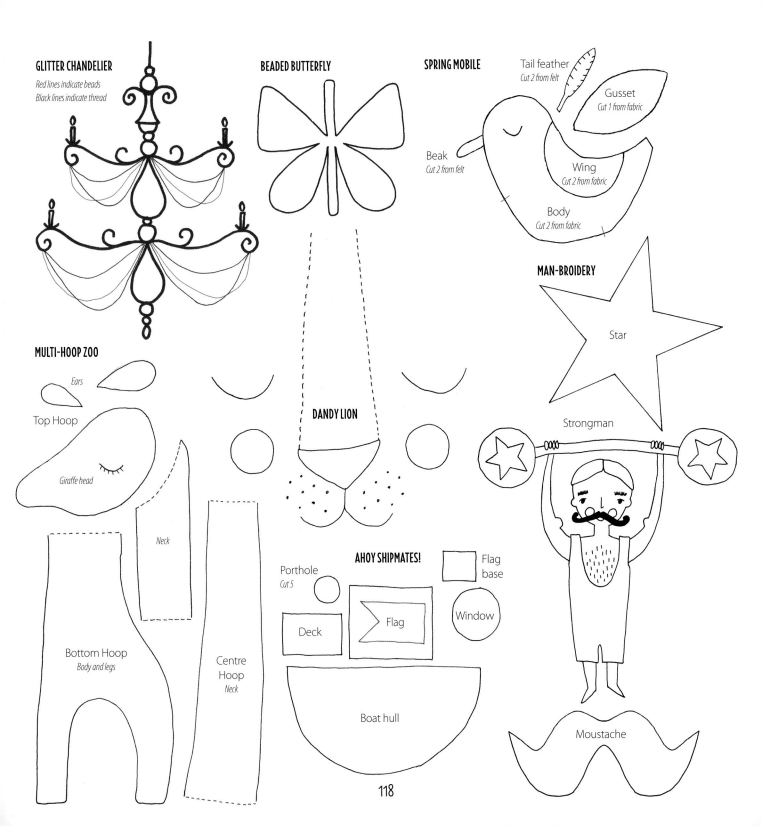

**GLITTER CHANDELIER**
*Red lines indicate beads*
*Black lines indicate thread*

**BEADED BUTTERFLY**

**SPRING MOBILE**

Tail feather
*Cut 2 from felt*

Gusset
*Cut 1 from fabric*

Beak
*Cut 2 from felt*

Wing
*Cut 2 from fabric*

Body
*Cut 2 from fabric*

**MAN-BROIDERY**

Star

Strongman

**MULTI-HOOP ZOO**

Ears

Top Hoop

Giraffe head

**DANDY LION**

Neck

Bottom Hoop
*Body and legs*

Centre
Hoop
*Neck*

**AHOY SHIPMATES!**

Porthole
*Cut 5*

Deck

Flag

Flag
base

Window

Boat hull

Moustache

118

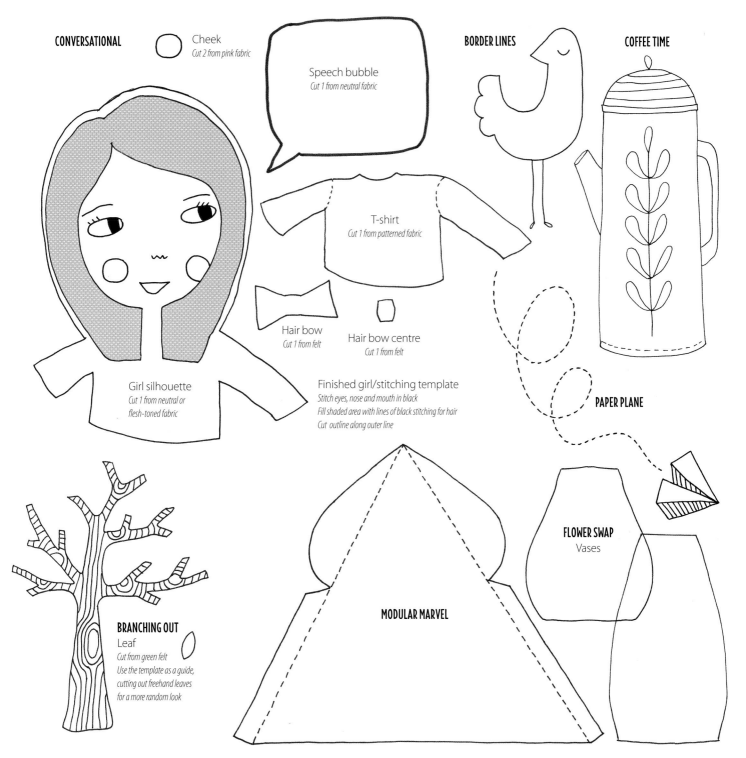

CONVERSATIONAL

Cheek
*Cut 2 from pink fabric*

Speech bubble
*Cut 1 from neutral fabric*

BORDER LINES

COFFEE TIME

T-shirt
*Cut 1 from patterned fabric*

Hair bow
*Cut 1 from felt*

Hair bow centre
*Cut 1 from felt*

Girl silhouette
*Cut 1 from neutral or
flesh-toned fabric*

Finished girl/stitching template
*Stitch eyes, nose and mouth in black*
*Fill shaded area with lines of black stitching for hair*
*Cut outline along outer line*

PAPER PLANE

BRANCHING OUT
Leaf
*Cut from green felt*
*Use the template as a guide,
cutting out freehand leaves
for a more random look*

MODULAR MARVEL

FLOWER SWAP
Vases

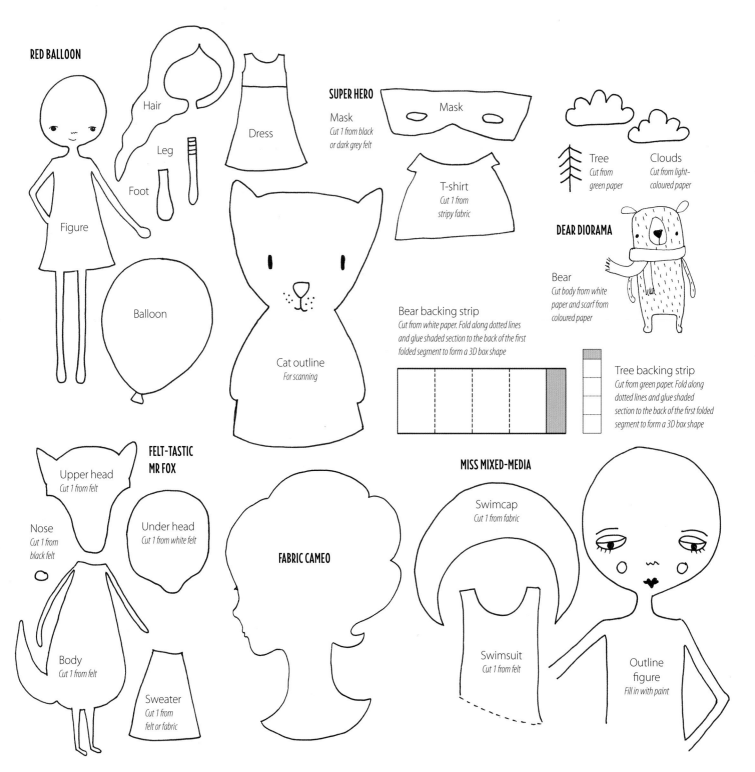

**RED BALLOON**

Hair

Leg

Foot

Figure

Balloon

Dress

**SUPER HERO**

Mask
*Cut 1 from black
or dark grey felt*

Mask

T-shirt
*Cut 1 from
stripy fabric*

Tree
*Cut from
green paper*

Clouds
*Cut from light-
coloured paper*

**DEAR DIORAMA**

Bear
*Cut body from white
paper and scarf from
coloured paper*

Cat outline
*For scanning*

Bear backing strip
*Cut from white paper. Fold along dotted lines
and glue shaded section to the back of the first
folded segment to form a 3D box shape*

Tree backing strip
*Cut from green paper. Fold along
dotted lines and glue shaded
section to the back of the first folded
segment to form a 3D box shape*

**FELT-TASTIC
MR FOX**

Upper head
*Cut 1 from felt*

Nose
*Cut 1 from
black felt*

Under head
*Cut 1 from white felt*

Body
*Cut 1 from felt*

Sweater
*Cut 1 from
felt or fabric*

**FABRIC CAMEO**

**MISS MIXED-MEDIA**

Swimcap
*Cut 1 from fabric*

Swimsuit
*Cut 1 from felt*

Outline
figure
*Fill in with paint*

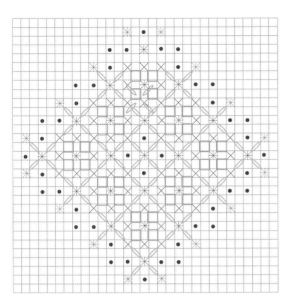

## CHICKEN SCRATCH
Stitch chart

| ✕ | Cross stitch |
| ✳ | Double cross stitch |
| • | French knot |
| ☐ | Woven circle (4 corners) |
| ◢ | Woven circle (2 corners) |

## MEGA STITCHING
Stitch Chart

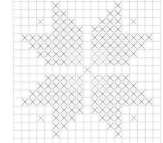

## CROSS STITCH REPEATS
Chevron pattern

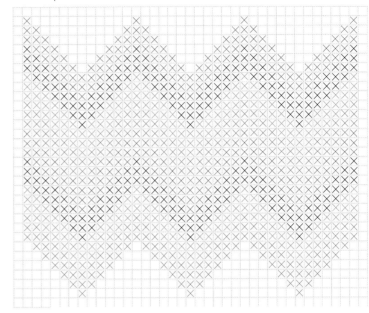

## REVERSE APPLIQUÉ    Leaves

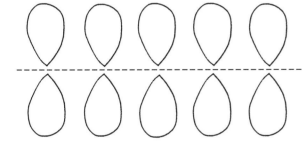

Seed heads

## CROSS STITCH REPEATS
Plaid pattern

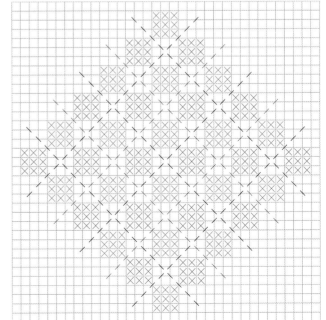

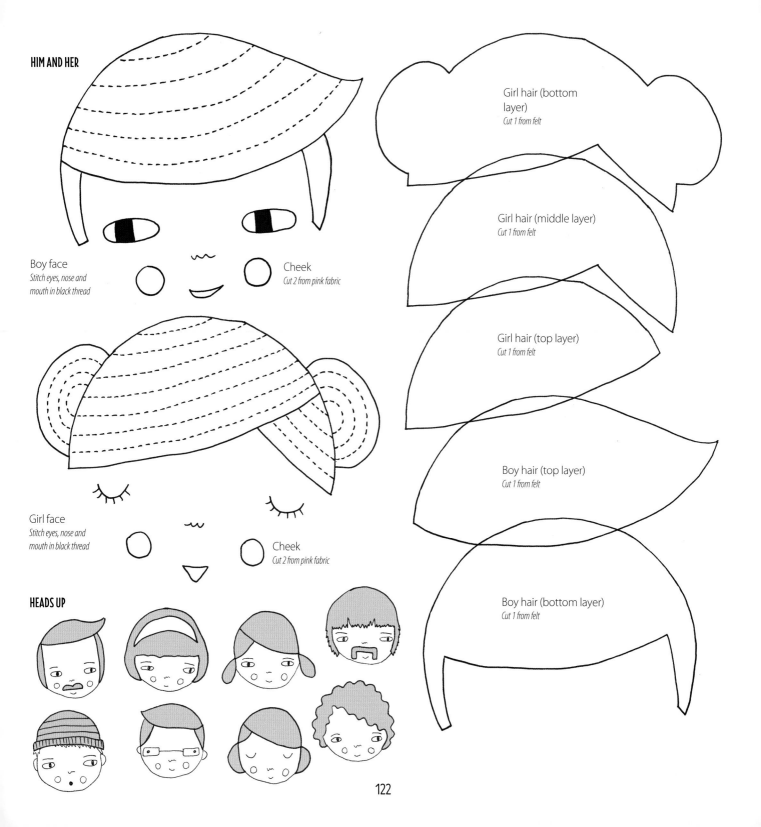

**HIM AND HER**

Boy face
*Stitch eyes, nose and mouth in black thread*

Cheek
*Cut 2 from pink fabric*

Girl face
*Stitch eyes, nose and mouth in black thread*

Cheek
*Cut 2 from pink fabric*

**HEADS UP**

Girl hair (bottom layer)
*Cut 1 from felt*

Girl hair (middle layer)
*Cut 1 from felt*

Girl hair (top layer)
*Cut 1 from felt*

Boy hair (top layer)
*Cut 1 from felt*

Boy hair (bottom layer)
*Cut 1 from felt*

122

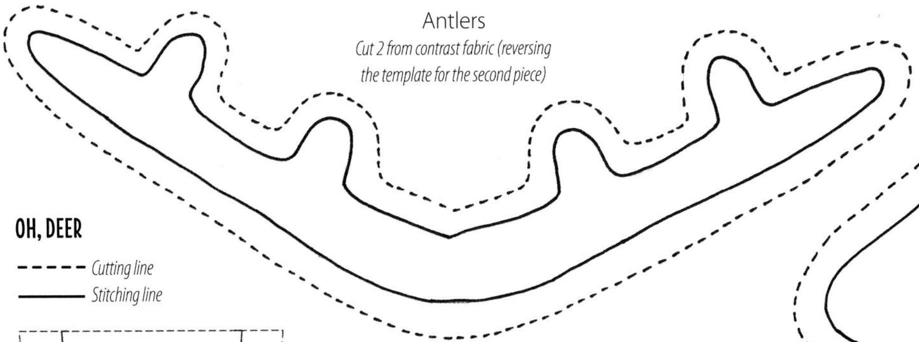

Antlers
*Cut 2 from contrast fabric (reversing the template for the second piece)*

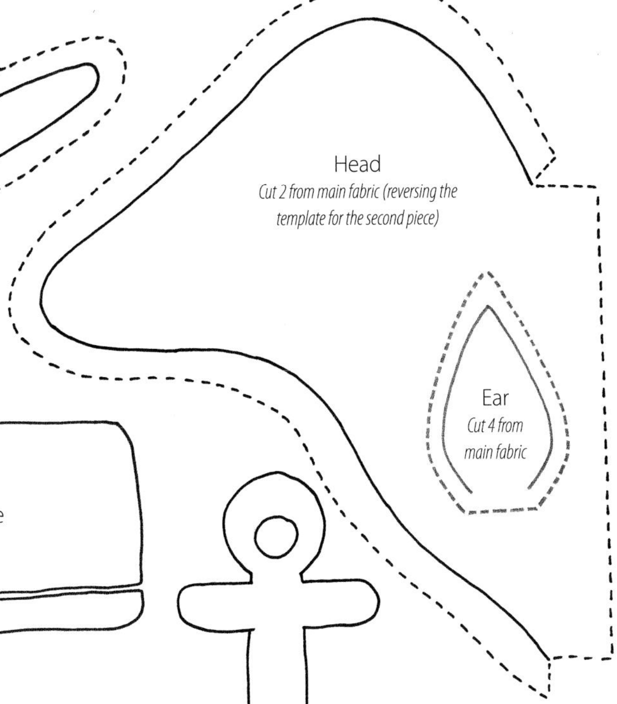

Head
*Cut 2 from main fabric (reversing the template for the second piece)*

**OH, DEER**

- - - *Cutting line*
――― *Stitching line*

Ear
*Cut 4 from main fabric*

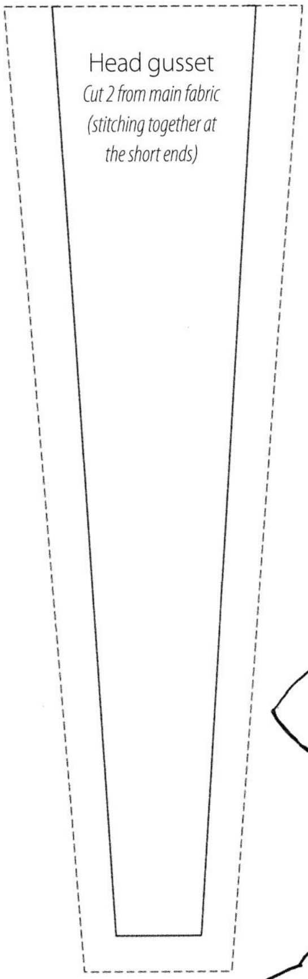

Head gusset
*Cut 2 from main fabric (stitching together at the short ends)*

**SIMPLE STENCILS**

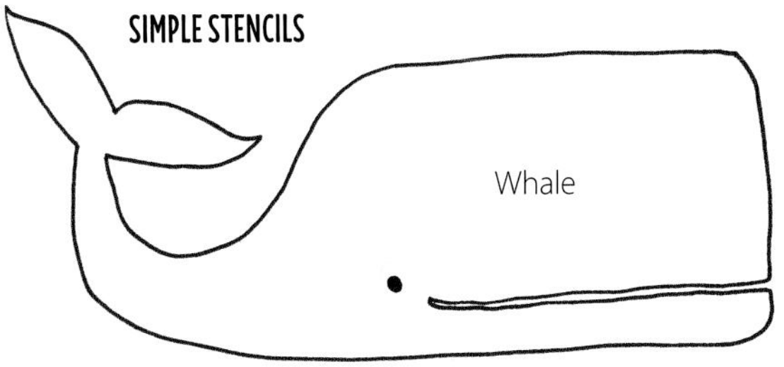

Whale

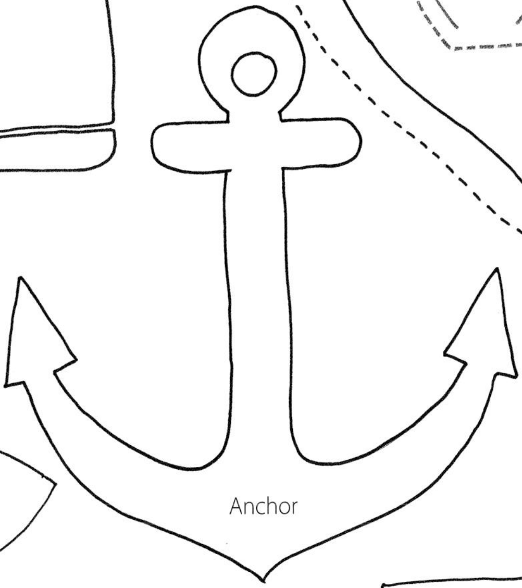

Anchor

Grass island
*Cut 1 from green felt or fabric*

**TO THE LIGHTHOUSE**

Sea scallops
*Cut 1 from blue fabric*
*Stitch the solid lines in white and the dotted lines in aqua*
*Copy this half of the template, flip it over and copy again for the other half*

Window
*Cut 2 or 3 from black felt*

Lighthouse cap
*Cut 1 from black felt*

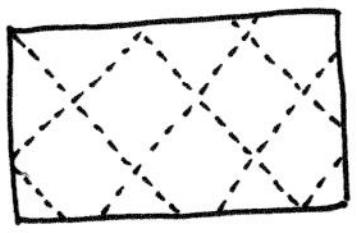

Light
*Cut 1 from light-coloured fabric*

Balcony
*Cut 1 from red felt*

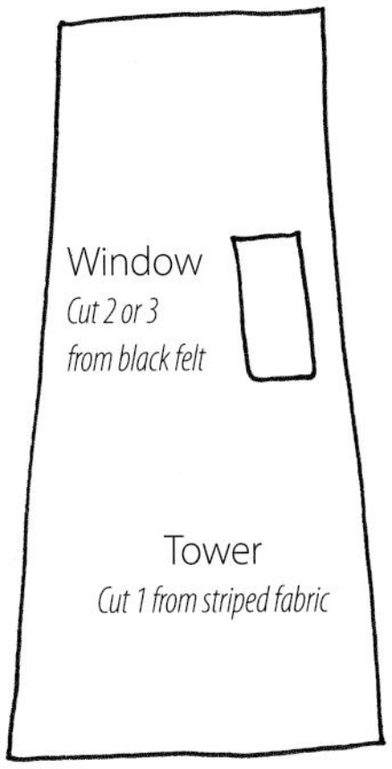

Tower
*Cut 1 from striped fabric*

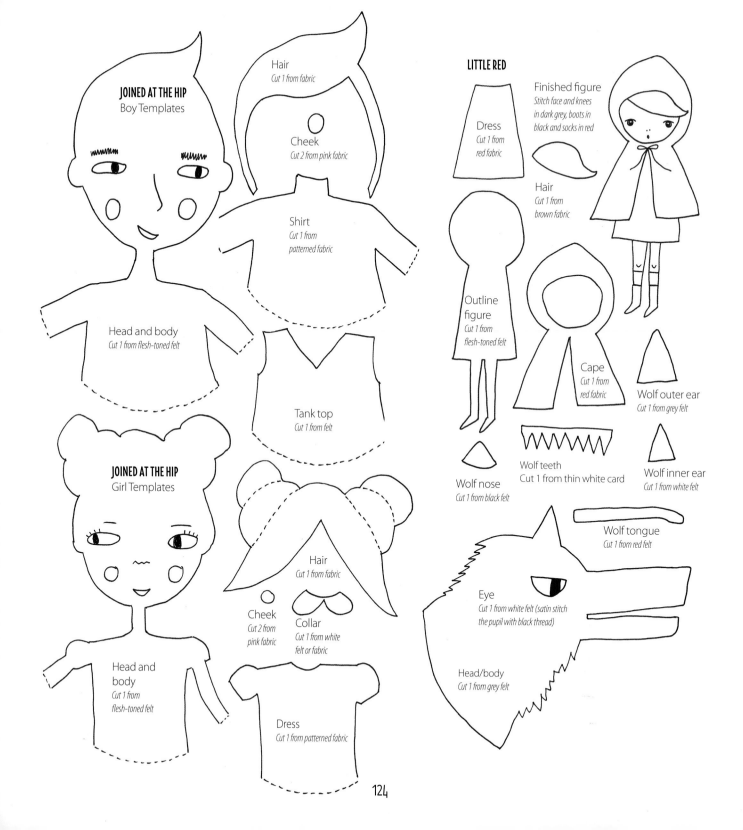

**JOINED AT THE HIP**
Boy Templates

Hair
*Cut 1 from fabric*

Cheek
*Cut 2 from pink fabric*

Shirt
*Cut 1 from patterned fabric*

Head and body
*Cut 1 from flesh-toned felt*

Tank top
*Cut 1 from felt*

**JOINED AT THE HIP**
Girl Templates

Hair
*Cut 1 from fabric*

Cheek
*Cut 2 from pink fabric*

Collar
*Cut 1 from white felt or fabric*

Head and body
*Cut 1 from flesh-toned felt*

Dress
*Cut 1 from patterned fabric*

**LITTLE RED**

Dress
*Cut 1 from red fabric*

Finished figure
*Stitch face and knees in dark grey, boots in black and socks in red*

Hair
*Cut 1 from brown fabric*

Outline figure
*Cut 1 from flesh-toned felt*

Cape
*Cut 1 from red fabric*

Wolf outer ear
*Cut 1 from grey felt*

Wolf inner ear
*Cut 1 from white felt*

Wolf teeth
*Cut 1 from thin white card*

Wolf nose
*Cut 1 from black felt*

Wolf tongue
*Cut 1 from red felt*

Eye
*Cut 1 from white felt (satin stitch the pupil with black thread)*

Head/body
*Cut 1 from grey felt*

124

FRENCH SHADING

HELLO OWL

MATRYOSHKA

Dress (upper)
Cut 1 from patterned fabric

Dress (upper)
Cut 1 from patterned fabric

Dress (lower)
Cut 1 from contrast patterned fabric
Add a strip of ribbon across the join
between upper and lower dress

Hood
Cut 1 from felt

Hood
Cut 1 from felt

Dress (lower)
Cut 1 from contrast patterned fabric
Add a strip of ribbon across the join
between upper and lower dress

Body
Cut 1 from neutral or
flesh-toned fabric

Body
Cut 1 from neutral or
flesh-toned fabric

Hood
Cut 1 from felt

Hood
Cut 1 from felt

Body
Cut 1 from neutral or
flesh-toned fabric

Body
Cut 1 from neutral or
flesh-toned fabric

Dress (lower)
Cut 1 from contrast patterned fabric
Add a strip of ribbon across the join
between upper and lower dress

Dress (lower)
Cut 1 from contrast
patterned fabric
Add a strip of ribbon
across the join between
upper and lower dress

Dress (upper)
Cut 1 from patterned fabric

Dress (upper)
Cut 1 from patterned fabric

# SUPPLIERS

**Beadworks**
21a Tower Street, London WC2H 9N, UK
Tel: 0207 240 0931
www.beadworks.co.uk
*Beads, crimps, invisible beading
thread and jewellery findings*

**Crafty Computer Paper**
Hamilton House, Mountain Road,
Leicester LE4 9HQ, UK
Tel: 0116 2744755
www.craftycomputerpaper.co.uk
*Specialist printing surfaces, including
T-shirt transfers and inkjet fabric sheets*

**The Cotton Patch**
1283–1285 Stratford Road, Hall Green,
Birmingham B28 9AJ, UK
Tel: 0121 702 2840
www.cottonpatch.co.uk
*Haberdashery and quilting supplies, including
fusible web, interfacing, freezer paper,
wadding and erasable marker pens*

**The Eternal Maker**
41 Terminus Rd, Chichester, West
Sussex PO19 8TX, UK
Tel: 01243 788174
www.eternalmaker.com
*Huge selection of fabrics, including wool
felt in a great range of colours*

**Home Crafts Direct**
Hamilton House, Mountain Road,
Leicester, LE4 9HQ, UK
Tel: 0116 2744755
www.homecrafts.co.uk
*Cyanotype fabric, screenprinting
medium and clock parts*

**John Lewis**
Tel: 08456 049049
*General craft supplies, including embroidery hoops,
yarn, counted-thread fabric and fancy buttons*

**MacCulloch & Wallis**
25–26 Dering Street, London W1S 1AT, UK
Tel: 020 7629 0311
www.macculloch-wallis.co.uk
*Feathers, faux flowers, coloured elastic
and other haberdashery*

**Papermaze**
Grange Farm, Otley, Ipswich, Suffolk IP6 9NS, UK
Tel: 01473 892195
www.papermaze.co.uk
*Papercraft supplies, including Mod Podge*

**Purl Soho**
459 Broome Street, New York, NY 10013, USA
Tel: 212-420-8796
www.purlsoho.com
*Embroidery hoops, notions, thread, yarn
and a fantastic selection of fabrics*

**Quilt Me Happy**
www.quiltmehappy.co.uk
*Polyester stuffing, crushed walnut shells,
blackboard fabric, plus quilting fabrics*

**Stitch Craft Create**
Brunel House, Forde Close, Newton
Abbot, Devon TQ12 4PU, UK
Tel: 0844 880 5852
www.stitchcraftcreate.co.uk
*Embroidery hoops, thread, crochet hooks,
Decopatch patterned tissue paper, yarn and fabric*

**Superbuzzy**
1794 East Main Street, Ventura, CA 93001, USA
Tel: 805-643-4143
www.superbuzzy.com
*Japanese fabrics, buttons, trims,
yarn and fun notions*

**Two Peas in a Bucket**
Tel: 888-896-7327
www.twopeasinabucket.com
*Papercraft materials, including chipboard
letters and numbers, rub-on transfers, patterned
paper, ink, stamps and paper flowers*

**V V Rouleaux**
102 Marylebone Lane, London, W1U 2QD, UK
Tel:  020 7224 5179
www.vvrouleaux.com
*Fancy braids, ribbons, trims and silk butterflies*

# Websites

**Cute Tape**
www.cutetape.com
*Decorative tapes, including washi,
fabric, paper, glitter and lace*

**Julie Kirk**
www.juliekirk.etsy.com
*Interesting packs of vintage paper for collage*

**Kitschy Digitals**
www.kitschydigitals.com
*Printable patterned papers and digital elements*

**Namolio**
www.namolio.com
*Crocheted flowers and beautiful linen yarn*

# ABOUT THE AUTHOR

Kirsty Neale is a freelance writer, illustrator and prolific designer-maker, living in London. She specializes in fabric and paper crafts, and enjoys combining new materials with vintage or repurposed finds. She has wide-ranging skills in many crafts and her work has been published in numerous books, including *State of Craft* and the David & Charles title *101 Ways to Stitch, Craft, Create*. Her inventive creations are also seen in magazines, including *Mollie Makes*. She writes a popular creative blog at: kirstyneale.typepad.com. For more on Kirsty see her website: www.kirstyneale.co.uk

# ACKNOWLEDGMENTS

With huge thanks to the team at D&C, including Jeni, Anna, Sarah and Lin, for their vision, guidance, patience and hoop-ish enthusiasm; to Shimelle and Alice for their helping hands; to my family and friends for love and vintage fabric; and to Steve – cheerleader, hand-holder, dinner-cooker and brave haberdashery-shopper. You are amazing.

Special thanks also to Jill and Louise at Hus & Hem (www.husandhem.co.uk), to Harlequin (www.harlequin.uk.com) and to Fifty One Percent/Pip Studio (www.pipstudio.com/en) for providing the beautiful props and wallpapers used throughout this book.

# INDEX

**A DAVID & CHARLES BOOK**

© F&W Media International, Ltd 2013

David & Charles is an imprint of F&W Media International, Ltd
Brunel House, Forde Close, Newton Abbot, TQ12 4PU, UK

F&W Media International, Ltd is a subsidiary of F+W Media, Inc
10151 Carver Road, Suite #200, Blue Ash, OH 45242, USA

Text and Designs © Kirsty Neale 2013
Layout and Photography © F&W Media International, Ltd 2013

First published in the UK and USA in 2013
Kirsty Neale has asserted her right to be identified as author of this work in
accordance with the Copyright, Designs and Patents Act, 1988.

The author and publisher have made every effort to ensure that all the instructions in the book are accurate and safe, and
therefore cannot accept liability for any resulting injury, damage or loss to persons or property, however it may arise.

Names of manufacturers and product ranges are provided for the information of
readers, with no intention to infringe copyright or trademarks.

A catalogue record for this book is available from the British Library.

ISBN-13: 978-1-4463-0298-9 paperback
ISBN-10: 1-4463-0298-9 paperback

Printed in China by RR Donnelley for
F&W Media International, Ltd
Brunel House, Forde Close, Newton Abbot, TQ12 4PU, UK

10 9 8 7 6 5 4 3 2 1

Editor: Jeni Hennah
Project Editor: Lin Clements
Junior Art Editor: Anna Fazakerley
Photographers:  Jack Kirby, Jack Gorman and Karl Adamson
Senior Production Controller: Kelly Smith

F+W Media publishes high quality books on a wide range of subjects.
For more great book ideas visit: **www.stitchcraftcreate.co.uk**